UNICORN
TEARS

UNICORN TEARS

WHY STARTUPS FAIL
AND HOW TO AVOID IT

JAMIE PRIDE

WILEY

First published in 2018 by John Wiley & Sons Australia, Ltd
42 McDougall St, Milton Qld 4064
Office also in Melbourne

Typeset in 13/15pt Arno Pro

© John Wiley & Sons Australia, Ltd 2018

The moral rights of the author have been asserted

A catalogue record for this book is available from the National Library of Australia

Cover design by Wiley

Cover images: © Evgenii141/iStockphoto-Rainbow,
© 123dartist/iStockphoto-Water Drop

10 9 8 7 6 5 4 3 2 1

Disclaimer

For Sam, Phoebe, Harrison and Imogen

CONTENTS

Unicorn: a technology startup company that reaches a $1 billion market value as determined by private or public investment.

Unicorn tears: the 92 per cent of technology startups that fail within the first three years of launch.

ABOUT THE AUTHOR

Jamie Pride is a serial entrepreneur and venture capitalist on a mission to help build better founders and a better venture capital ecosystem to support them.

As an entrepreneur, Jamie sold his first startup, Velteo, to New York–based system integrator Bluewolf, and has founded six technology startups. As an investor, he has raised more than $16 million in funding for startups via private and public markets, including completing an IPO on the Australian Stock Exchange in 2015.

He has more than 20 years' experience with international technology and digital media organisations, including leading realestate.com.au and senior positions with Deloitte Digital, salesforce.com, Red Hat, Veritas and Cisco Systems.

Jamie is also a sought-after public speaker and regularly comments on startups, entrepreneurship, venture capital, disruptive innovation and design thinking.

He is the managing partner at Phi Digital Ventures, an early-stage, social impact venture fund that seeks to invest in Australian companies looking to change the world. He is also the co-founder of The Founder Lab, an educational institution for entrepreneurs that seeks to build and support better founders.

Having worked extensively as both an entrepreneur and an investor he has a unique insight into what it takes to make a startup successful and what it takes to get funded.

INTRODUCTION
THERE HAS TO BE A BETTER WAY!

Over the past 20 years I have founded and funded numerous technology startups. During that time I have seen a clear pattern emerging: startup failure has become an accepted industry norm, and it has an impact that reaches far beyond financial loss to investors. Having experienced my own journey of failure as a founder more than once, I have felt the very real, deep, personal impact of that failure on me, my family and my colleagues.

As I sat at home, licking my wounds from my most recent startup failure, the thought of writing this book took hold — and it soon became an obsession for me. I started talking to founders, and what they shared with me didn't surprise me at all. Many of the first-time founders I spoke to were lost, with no map to guide them; even the more experienced founders, burnt out or stressed out, felt alone, isolated, with nowhere to turn for support. I was determined to write a book on startup failure *by a founder for founders*.

I quickly discovered that startup failure is ingrained in the ecosystem. Concepts such as 'fail fast', misunderstood and misapplied, are thrown around without much thought. The traditional venture capitalist approach to failure is to place a lot of bets on the understanding that, while most ventures will fail, a very few may turn out to be 'unicorns' and return vast profits that will make up for all the losses. It is a very wasteful approach.

The financial waste in failed startups is fairly widely understood; less recognised is the largely unspoken issue of human waste. I've seen the dark side of startups: 49 per cent of founders in one survey reported some kind of mental health issue. By their own admission, more than 30 per cent of founders have experienced depression while 27 per cent have suffered serious anxiety. Founders are fatigued!

But isn't the startup game meant to be fun, exciting and glamorous? Don't we keep seeing successful startup founders smiling on the front pages of the business press, having completed their latest triumphant capital raising or IPO? The culture of 'I'm crushing it' makes it hard for founders to admit they are struggling.

The irony is that most startup failure is preventable. In its simplest form, startup failure is often a consequence of 'self-harm': rather than crumbling in the face of overwhelming external competition, startups typically implode. This is good news, because it means you can do something about it!

There is a better way. In this book you will learn:

- ▶ the three elements of startup DNA and how each one contributes to failure
- ▶ the 10 key reasons why startups fail
- ▶ how to become a fit founder, and why capacity is more important than capability
- ▶ how to develop the core founder characteristics of resilience, awareness and adaptability
- ▶ the myths that surround startups and how to bust them
- ▶ why Hollywood got it right, and the parallels between making a movie and founding a startup

- the Hollywood Method™, a structured approach to founding and building a startup

- the importance of investor-centred design, and how to develop your funding fitness program

- The 5 Ps of funding fitness and a surefire way to get your startup funded by the right investors, at the right valuation, in the shortest possible time.

So why should you listen to me? What do I know about startups? Well, in short, I've made a lot of mistakes so you don't have to. I have gone through the personal pain of startup failure. I've felt the sting of losing investors' money and the embarrassment and stress of large-scale public failure. And I'm still here. I can teach you the lessons I've learned firsthand.

Not only am I a founder, but I am also a venture capitalist. This gives me a unique perspective. I have sat on both sides of the table and have insights into how each player in the game thinks. I truly love what I do, and I am on a mission to help build better founders and a better venture capital ecosystem to support them.

You might say I am a misfit. I hope you can identify with that. Most founders I know are nonconformists. They don't thrive in the corporate world. They are passionately committed to bringing their ideas into the world, but they are struggling. It doesn't have to be that way. Founding a startup should be one of the most rewarding, exciting and challenging things you do in your life. I hope reading this book will help you enjoy those rewards and avoid your own unicorn tears.

CHAPTER 1
COUNTING THE COST

———

More than 100 million startups are founded every year (that's about three every second), but 92 per cent of them will fail within three years — and the crazy thing is that this is largely preventable.

Just think about that for a second. In any other area of your business or personal life, if 92 times out of 100 a course of action didn't work, you'd think of doing something quite different. Yet in the startup world these high failure rates are accepted with a shrug, because 'that's how it is'. Why?

This book aims to challenge that acceptance. Failure shouldn't be the natural way of things.

We need to study startup failure more closely to understand why it happens. That's what struck me when I started investing in startups. If we can better understand why and how startups fail, then we can increase the chances of their success. By learning from others' mistakes, we can ensure we don't repeat them. If we can move the needle to decrease the failure rate by just a small amount, it will have a huge impact — both to the founders who put their heart and soul into their startups and to the investors who back them.

Paul Graham, the respected venture capitalist and co-founder of Y Combinator, distinguishes between startups that are *default dead* (if they maintain their current trajectory on sales, growth rates, expenses, they will run out of cash) and those that are *default alive*. The reality is that most startups, especially in the early stages, are default dead. Many founders don't even ask this question, or they ask it way too late. Graham goes on to describe the 'fatal pinch', where a startup is default dead, unable to raise the cash to survive, essentially the 'walking dead'. The founders are deluded into thinking they can raise more cash, but they are essentially in a death spiral. Raising capital is by no means easy or certain, and even for those who do manage it, fundraising success does not equate to future success. Especially if the company is default dead.

Default alive, on the other hand, means a startup is at or heading to break-even and can survive and thrive on its available cash. These businesses have a viable future, and can move on from thinking about fundraising to thinking about growth and new prospects. I want to help founders think about the default state of their startup, and to consider why and how it could fail.

THE CULT OF FAILURE

Failure is a word you hear a lot in the startup community. The term *fail fast* is associated with the lean startup movement, which is very well articulated by Eric Ries in his book *The Lean Startup*. However, I believe the term is much overused in the startup community and indeed misunderstood by many founders and their teams.

Behind the *lean startup* is the concept of iteration. The idea is that if a new product proves to be unsuccessful, the business should let it fail fast, after which the product can be iterated based on customer testing and feedback. You develop a *minimum viable product* (in which you invest the least expense needed to make it workable), and you test it with customers. You iterate and improve it, then repeat the cycle.

It is a sensible approach, but it is often misunderstood by founders. What Ries is talking about in *The Lean Startup* is a robust approach to product development and a way of validating product/market fit. Let's get some customer feedback, then we'll test, iterate, test, iterate, and we'll go through that product cycle. The challenge is that founders often misconstrue the fail fast idea by applying it at the company level.

Ries doesn't mean that your startup should fail. He is talking about iteration and customer feedback loops at a product level. The startup community gravitates towards these catchphrases and sound bites that don't mean much outside their proper context. Your startup still needs a plan.

I'm all for developing a learning culture inside a startup and truly practising the ideas behind the lean startup, but I want to define the difference between good failure and bad failure.

SELF-HARM: GOOD FAILURE VS BAD FAILURE

Most founders think about failure as an 'external' event — something that happens to you, causing you to fail. More often failure is an 'internal' event. It's about self-harm: you are doing something or not doing something that causes you to fail. Sadly, most startups fail from the inside.

The insight here is recognising that it's not about karma or fate. Most startups are disruptive to some extent: it is they who are delivering external competitive pressure to traditional businesses, not the other way around. Most startups are not disrupted by someone else — they implode. And guess what? That's great news, because it means you can develop a plan and take action yourself to avoid failure.

Later I will discuss the 10 main reasons why startups fail. Every single one of those reasons can be prevented. There is a belief that startups defy gravity. We have this twisted idea that startups are somehow special, but the truth is this: a startup is no more special than any small business. If I intended to start a small business such as a bakery or a café it would be reasonable to be asked, 'Do you have a sales plan? Do you have a marketing plan? Have you thought about where you're going to locate it and the demographics of your customers?' Many startup founders, however, think they don't need a plan. They are just going to 'fail fast'. No shit. The startup myth perpetuates the view that gravity does not apply to them. In fact, they need all the planning and execution that any small business needs.

PLACE YOUR BETS: THE VENTURE CAPITALIST APPROACH TO FAILURE

Venture capitalists (VCs) understand very well the risks associated with investing in technology startups and have developed a simple but effective approach to managing that risk. The conventional VC approach to risk mitigation is to invest in a broad portfolio of startups. VCs traditionally came from finance backgrounds. Before and during the internet bubble, they funded startups with little understanding of the companies or business models they were investing in. They knew there were high failure rates, and their approach was 'let's just lay a lot of bets'.

The premise was if 92 out of 100 startups fail, then put down 100 bets and the eight successes need to pay off big enough to make up for the failures (and they did). In a world of unicorns, the eight paid off at rates that were so high that it made the 92 failures insignificant — except to their founders.

It was a reasonable strategy from the VC point of view. Let's just lay out a whole lot of bets, assume that 92 of them are going to fail, and make sure the eight are unicorns.

Today VCs are far more sophisticated. They are more involved with the companies they invest in (many of them are former entrepreneurs and startup founders), and far more interested in examining the reasons for failure and mitigating them. If you look at the problem from a venture capital perspective, there's an absolute economic reason to improve the success rate of startups — investor return. More success equals more money for everyone.

That said, a lot of investing behaviour, particularly at the early stage, is still very much influenced by what I call the *slot-machine effect*.

THE SLOT-MACHINE EFFECT

Human behaviour is a funny thing, especially when it comes to payoffs. Everyone knows that you can't win at the slot machines, that they are wired and programmed for you to lose — casinos were not built by the winners. Everyone knows the statistics, but people play them anyway. Imagine 100 people playing slot machines; 92 of them pull the handle, and 92 lose their money. Then eight people sitting near them pull the handle and make a billion dollars. Human behaviour doesn't look at that in a rational, statistical way.

It's the same reason people play the lottery. Even though people know the chances of winning are minuscule, the jackpots are so enormous that they create a reality distortion field. People don't think rationally about the losses.

When people see an Uber, a Facebook, an Instagram or an Atlassian — all high-profile startups — they put them on a pedestal. There's a lot of cultural storytelling about those businesses, which has created a powerful mythology. In fact these companies are rare exceptions to the rule, yet humans have this inbuilt emotional belief that says, 'If I want it badly enough, I'm going to be one of the exceptions.'

I listen to three or four startup pitches almost every week. Most people who pitch to me haven't addressed the core, foundational issues around avoiding startup failure. They don't have a business model. They don't have a value proposition for a product or service that customers will pay for. It's astounding.

I meet prospective founders all the time who say (and believe), 'I've got an excellent idea — it's going to be the next Facebook.' That's easier said than done. There's a big journey between a brilliant idea and Facebook. Too many founders don't recognise that or they minimise in their minds how challenging the necessary execution around an idea is.

UNICORN TEARS: THE REAL IMPACT OF FAILURE

It's easy to think about the financial impact of failure. Millions of dollars of investors' money is flushed away every time a startup goes under. Billions of dollars are wasted every year. As a founder myself, I have also seen the results of failure on another level — the personal impact. I've seen founders whose marriages have broken up, founders who suffer from depression, founders who have turned to alcohol or drugs, or have even become suicidal. This is the dark side of startups that no one wants to talk about. We love to focus on the glamour and the unicorns, but not on the unicorn tears.

Startup failures take a huge personal toll on founders. They have taken a risk, put themselves out there, worked themselves to the bone, then the business goes under, usually in a very public way. They must go home and tell their partner that they don't know how they're going to make the mortgage payments or the school fees. They have lost their job, and the rest of their team have lost their jobs too.

This is the reason I wrote this book, and it's something I am hugely passionate about. By addressing the preventable failure of startups, and the impact this failure has on founders, I want to help you to avoid the unicorn tears.

We should be concerned with investors losing their money, it has a huge impact on the economy. But we should also be concerned with founder waste. For our society to progress we need innovators and risk-takers. We need startup founders. Too many of those innovators are wasted, chewed up and spat out, never to return to the startup ecosystem. Some may say this is Darwinism at work, that only the strong survive. Yet most founders simply aren't equipped with the skills they need to be successful, and we are only now starting to explore and understand why startups fail and how to prevent that. I want those founders, having learned from their mistakes, to come back and build bigger and better startups.

CASE STUDY: MY 'CLIPP' AROUND THE EAR

Several years ago I made an investment in an early-stage startup called Clipp. It is a business operating in the mobile payments space, solving the problem of bar tab management. To use Clipp you go to a bar, open a bar tab using the mobile app, order drinks and pay automatically. It is a very smooth, Uber-like experience.

When I met the company founders I was excited. It was one of the few startups I saw that year to do something new. They had built a functional version of the product, and it was working 'in the wild'. The technology was unbelievably well built and the software developers in the business were amazing. I was one of a group of investors who seed-funded the business, representing approximately 27 per cent of the equity and taking a seat on the board.

(continued)

CASE STUDY: MY 'CLIPP' AROUND THE EAR (CONT'D)

In retrospect, if I look at the reasons for startup failure that I will discuss in detail in these pages, I think this business ticked almost every box. In my view there were founder issues and funding issues, and the business model turned out to have major challenges.

There were a lot of arguments. From an investor perspective, I would say that the founders were difficult to coach in the way I would have hoped. By this I mean lots of people with experience were trying to help the founders of the company, but that help wasn't well received. The founding team argued among themselves too. They were all really nice people personally, but I feel that the dynamic between them, and ultimately with us as investors, deteriorated — to the detriment of the company.

From a funding perspective, we probably gave them too much money in a single tranche. And we didn't link the funding to key operational milestones. More importantly, even though it was a sexy product, in my view the business model had serious challenges. It just wasn't possible to make enough money using the business model we had. The model had made that business default dead. It came close to running out of funding (the fatal pinch) and another strategic investor took on our investment. The initial seed investors lost a reasonable amount of money.

Clipp was one of my earliest investments. I made a lot of mistakes. That said, the experience was a major inspiration for this book. After my investment in and subsequent exit from Clipp, I reflected a lot on why the business didn't achieve its full potential, and what I could have done differently. Many of the lessons outlined in this book come from what I learned from that investment. It was then that I began to look more deeply into why startups fail and the various levers that you can pull to prevent it.

In the aftermath there were a lot of questions. Could we have foreseen the founder dynamic? Could we have done more due diligence around identifying the risks? Could we have put more effort into validating the business model before we made our investment? Could we have helped the founders validate their business model? How could we have partnered with the founders more effectively around some of the issues — their cash burn rate, for example — so the business was more successful? It was a business with so much promise — more than I'd seen in a long time. Sadly that promise was just not realised, largely because of preventable, internally driven issues.

It's easy to underestimate the huge personal impact of these failures, when you have investors breathing down your neck and unhappy customers, and the embarrassment of telling your friends and family, 'Hey my business isn't going well — it may go under.'

The problems weigh heavily on you when things aren't going well, so it wasn't a good experience for those founders. But investors can move on and make another investment. It's not the same for those who put their blood, sweat and tears into the business.

LIGHT AT THE END OF THE TUNNEL

By now you are probably thinking, 'Why would I ever want to get into this startup game? It sounds horrible.' Ask any founder and they will tell you how hard the journey is — but also how rewarding. Creating something from an idea, and turning it into a successful company, is hugely satisfying — *if* you have the capacity and capability to take on that challenge. I want to introduce you to a methodical approach to developing yourself as a founder and building a startup that works.

You will face many challenges as a startup founder. Hiring is important, but this isn't a book about talent management. Leadership is essential, but this isn't a book about leadership. There are many dimensions to success in business. In this book I am looking at how you can avoid, prevent or mitigate mistakes that would have a high impact on your success or failure. I set out a structured methodology for how to develop your product from an idea to a fully launched company with the maximum chance of success, while making sure you as a founder survive the journey.

Startup success isn't an art, let alone a black art. And it isn't a matter of saying, let's just roll the dice and hope it works. Taking a structured approach to managing startup risk gives you a critical competitive advantage. By reducing some of the risks, you're going to jump ahead of other startups.

Since the internet bubble, technology startups have proliferated at an extraordinary rate (as mentioned earlier, three startups are founded every second). More than $50 billion is invested in venture capital every year. While that sounds like a lot of money, with more competition for a finite amount of money, startup capital is in fact becoming harder to find. In particular, seed funding (to get started) and 'Series A' funding (to grow) are becoming more difficult to access because investors know that a lot of startups are going to fail. By studying why failure occurs and how to mitigate those risks you improve your odds of being funded.

You need to be able to have an informed conversation with potential investors: 'We know most startups fail, but here's why they do, and here's what we're doing to eliminate those failure points.' With this informed approach, investors are going to take you more seriously. Thinking more deeply about failure *before* it occurs means you're going to be more prepared when issues arise, and this will set you apart from the many founders who don't even understand that their startup is default dead.

Myth: Startups are glamorous

Do you know a startup founder? If you don't, I want you to go out and find one. Once you have found one (the hoodie is often a giveaway), ask them about their experience as a startup founder. You will hear words such as *exciting, stressful, fun, challenging* and *enlightening*. What you won't hear is *glamorous*. If you expect founding a startup to be glamorous, then you should put this book down and go back to your corporate job. Startups aren't for you.

ARE YOU STARING FAILURE IN THE FACE?

Before you begin your startup journey it's worth asking yourself some important questions. Here are 10 questions you should think about.

1. What is your motivation for starting your business?

2. What proof do you have that customers *want* your product?

3. What proof do you have that customers *will pay* for your product?

4. How long have you known your co-founders? Do you need them?

5. Have you ever had an argument with your co-founders? Are you friends?

6. What unique skills do your co-founders bring? Could you just hire someone instead?

7. Have you built a startup before? What do you think it will be like?

8. How do you react to criticism? How do you deal with stress or pressure?

9. What kind of investors do you want?

10. What will you say to your investors if you lose all their money?

Having rational, honest conversations with all your stakeholders before you start is critical.

On a personal level, discussing your fears and expectations with friends and family will help. What support will you need from them? If you have a significant other, talk it through with them. Discuss the risks, time commitments and potential for stress. Address your fears and what support you may need.

Even more important is to have a frank discussion with your potential business partners and co-founders. Are you all aligned to the same values? Do you have a common motivation for starting the business? Will they run when the chips are down? What will you do if things go wrong? What will you do if things go right? What if someone wants to get out of the business and the others don't? Do you even need your co-founders? Would it be easier just to hire the skills that one or all of them bring? Or do they bring unique skills that earn them an equity position? Set expectations up front.

Talk to your investors. Discuss the risks. A common mistake that founders make is to gloss over the ugly parts. Most investors can tell. The smart ones know the risky nature of investing in early-stage businesses. You gain far more credibility if you have realistic and honest conversations with your investors than if you try to sugar-coat it. Discuss your plans and how you intend to mitigate the potential risks. Consider what help you need from them. Involve them in the business. Use their networks and experience. You don't have to do this alone, and when you engage them in the company they will feel far more comfortable about their investment in you and the business.

Lastly, talk to other founders. Build a solid network of people who are facing the same challenges as you and can act as a sounding board. Most startups face common problems. Tapping into the experience of others can fast-track your learning and give you insights into how to solve your current challenges.

OVER TO YOU
3 STEPS TO STARTUP SUCCESS

Success starts with you. Here are some steps you can take to set yourself on the right path.

STEP 1: QUESTION YOUR MOTIVES

Why are you starting this business? What is your motivation? Are you scratching an itch? Money motivates some people; some people say, 'It sounds cool' or 'I just want to be an entrepreneur'. Some people have a genuine passion for solving problems. There are a whole bunch of motivations behind startups and their founders. It's important to understand yours.

Your business needs a solid foundation, and that foundation is you. If your motivation is weak, then you will likely give up when the chips are down or when you face heavy criticism. Getting this right means you will be well placed for the challenges ahead. You need to be prepared. There will be failures. There will be stress. You will work your arse off. Reflect on your motivation and commitment. Do you want this? Why? How badly?

STEP 2: BECOME A STUDENT OF FAILURE

I have a horrible fear of flying, but I love watching the TV show *Air Crash Investigation*. Knowing that air accidents are analysed in such detail to prevent future crashes makes me more comfortable when flying.

Beyond this book, there is a mountain of information in the public domain about startup failure, and you can learn a lot from the autopsy. Go and read up on three high-profile startup failures and analyse them. What can you learn from them? Do any of the causes apply to your startup? Could the failure have been foreseen? What could they have done differently? Speak to founders who have failed in the past. Most founders I know are extremely open about their past mistakes.

STEP 3: FIND MENTORS

Entrepreneurs tell me that being a founder can be very lonely. Carrying the burden of responsibility for the success of the product, the team and the business can be a tough proposition. They have put their reputation on the line with investors and feel a huge weight on their shoulders. Not to mention the fear.

You don't have to do this alone. One of the amazing things about startups today is that there is this large, vibrant community that wants to see everyone succeed. Experienced entrepreneurs have already faced the challenges you will face. Seek them out. Ask for their opinion and advice. I strongly recommend creating an advisory board, either formally or informally. These advisers will be an essential source of mental and emotional support.

RECAP

Startups are awesome! But they need the right preparation. Many fail that don't have to. Startup failure is generally caused not by an external event, but by an internal one — they fail as a result of self-harm. Thoughtful study and analysis of the causes of failure will give your startup a critical competitive advantage and therefore a better chance of success.

Understanding that startup failure is common but not inevitable is the beginning of your journey to standing out from the crowd. When you have acknowledged, analysed and understood the risks and the failure modes, you will be more credible and knowledgeable when you speak with investors. Your evident competence will win you far more attention from venture capitalists and investors than first-timers who demonstrate less judgement.

Is your startup default dead or default alive? Call it early and act on it. By calling it now, your team will have a common language, and they will feel confident that your startup will be a greater success than others that appear to be just wandering in the wilderness. You will sleep better at night, and have less worry and anxiety, because you know you're planning for and controlling those common failure points.

WHAT'S NEXT?

Startup failure can be attributed to three common root causes: founders, funding and flawed business models. In the next chapter I will outline the 10 main reasons why startups fail, and why your MBA won't make you a successful startup founder.

CHAPTER 2
F IS FOR FAILURE

Before we can analyse startup failure we need a common understanding of what a startup is. In his book *The Startup Owner's Manual*, the respected educator and entrepreneur Steve Blank defines a startup as 'a temporary organisation in search of a scalable, repeatable, profitable business model'. Once a startup finds and successfully demonstrates a business model it transforms into a more structured corporation, and sadly loses some of its startup DNA.

What is the DNA of a startup? In its simplest form, a startup is a business that occupies a space at the intersection of three elements: founders, funding and business model (figure 2.1, overleaf):

- **Founders:** Someone has to do the work. Whether through a sole founder, a partnership or a hired team, startup success is usually heavily influenced by the people and personalities who work there — and those founders need to be fit enough to lead the business.

- **Funding:** Sooner or later (usually sooner), startups require capital in order to develop a product and go to market. That capital can come from bootstrapping a business yourself, from friends and family, or from venture capitalists. Regardless of the source, startups cannot survive without money.

▶ **Business model:** The seed of a startup is an idea, out of which grows a product and a business model. Most startups are defined by their idea; that said, this is usually the least important factor in their success. What is more important is solving a relevant problem and creating a value proposition that customers validate. We will talk a lot more about this.

FIGURE 2.1: ANATOMY OF A STARTUP

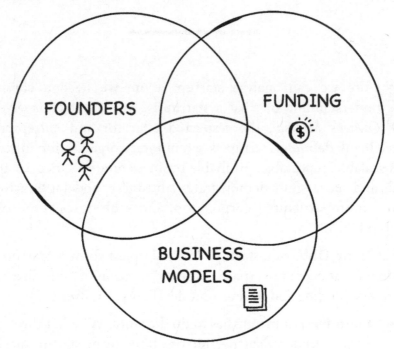

THE 3 Fs OF FAILURE

Fail in high school and you are usually graded an F; the same is true of startups. Depending on who you ask, there are a multitude of reasons why startups fail. Each strand of startup DNA contributes its own reasons for failure, but all of them relate directly to one of the 3 Fs (figure 2.2):

1. founder failures
2. funding failures
3. flawed business models.

You can't solve a problem you don't recognise or whose existence you deny. Acknowledging and understanding why startups fail is critical to success. It allows you to develop a plan.

FIGURE 2.2: WHY STARTUPS FAIL

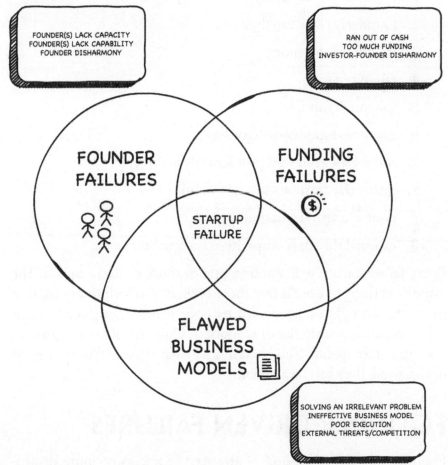

When I ask founders why startups fail, some show a degree of understanding, but many more have never even given it a thought. One of the inspiring things about founders is their drive and passion, but idealism can often blind them to the common causes of failure.

THE 10 MAIN REASONS WHY STARTUPS FAIL

Delving deeper into why startups fail, 10 primary reasons emerge:

1. founder(s) lack capacity
2. founder(s) lack capability
3. founder disharmony
4. ran out of cash
5. too much funding
6. investor–founder disharmony
7. solving an irrelevant problem (desirability)
8. ineffective business model (viability)
9. poor execution (feasibility)
10. external threats/competition (adaptability).

Every failed startup will manifest one or more of these causes. The important thing to note is that most of them can be influenced; that is, most such failures are caused by poor planning, a poor team or poor execution within the organisation. Only on rare occasions is a startup outcompeted. The good news is that if these failures can be understood, they can be avoided.

FOUNDER-DRIVEN FAILURES

Founders are the life blood of any startup and contribute dispro-portionately to their success or failure. If I asked you to think of a startup founder, you would most likely conjure up an image of someone like Steve Jobs or Mark Zuckerberg, yet such entrepreneurs are exceptions rather than the norm. Startup founders are of course as diverse as the ideas they build on. It has been estimated that there are more than 450 million entrepreneurs around the world who are working on startups in some form or another, and more are joining the community every day. These new founders are often poorly equipped for their journey. They confuse capacity and capability, and to build a successful startup they will need both.

Founder capacity is about how equipped a founder is to face the day-to-day challenges of running and leading a startup. This ranges across the spectrum from their physical fitness to their mental and emotional readiness. Capacity is like the fuel in the tank that allows you to make the journey. Many founders I see who struggle have not focused enough on building capacity; that is, they haven't taken care of or developed themselves enough.

Founder capability is more easily quantified and comprises the skills necessary to run a startup. This covers technical, communication, leadership, negotiation and conflict resolution skills. Capability is far easier to acquire than capacity, but I would suggest that capacity is more important for success.

It is also widely acknowledged that co-founders, or teams of founders, with complementary skills are more successful than single founders. Yet I have seen many startups implode because of founder disharmony. Choosing a co-founder and learning to work with them is critical. Surrounding yourself with the right people — from board members to advisers — will also have a significant impact on your success.

I have developed a founder fitness model that I will discuss in chapter 6. This model provides a structure for developing yourself as a founder. It focuses on helping founders build physical, mental and emotional capacity in order to be more successful.

A word on diversity

Startups are short on everything. There's never enough time, or money, and everyone needs to pull their weight. Maybe larger businesses can afford to tolerate some inefficiencies in the relationships between people and in the business model or processes. In a startup, you just can't afford to carry any underperforming team members. Working in a startup with an impressive group of people will be one of the best experiences of your life. Working with the wrong people will be a nightmare. The old image of startup leaders as hard-asses who don't collaborate — which was in part the personality of Apple's co-founder and CEO, Steve Jobs, for example, or at least that was the way the media portrayed him — has been debunked.

Startup teams need harmony and complementary skills. The idea of the 'Super Founder' has gone the way of the dodo. Instead, what has come to the forefront is diversity — in startups as well as in established businesses. Once, the startup was the domain of the white male. Today, we see better gender and ethnic diversity, a greater range of financial and cultural backgrounds, racial diversity — you name it, it's out there. This change is design-led and is a critical success factor. Diversity in your people brings a variety of ideas and thinking that produces better outcomes for investors.

FUNDING-DRIVEN FAILURES

Failure due to running out of money seems a pretty obvious one. Most failed startups eventually run out of money regardless of the root cause of the failure. This could be because investors have lost confidence in the founders or because the business model has not proven out. Ultimately the *fatal pinch* comes, at which point there is not enough time to raise additional capital before existing cash reserves run out.

Surprisingly a startup can also fail because it is overfunded. I liken this to giving a starving person a huge meal, causing them to die from overeating. Overfunded startups run the risk of losing their edge and their hustle. I have seen numerous well-funded startups take their foot off the gas and focus more on the new office fit-out and the design of their business cards than on continuing to prove out their customer hypotheses and value propositions. In my experience, there is a funding sweet spot for early-stage startups.

Just as founder disharmony can destroy a startup, so can founder– investor disharmony. It is crucial that you choose the right investors and that you bring those investors along for the journey. Having investors breathing down your neck every step of the way or being misaligned for the future direction of the business is something a startup and its founders can well do without.

As a founder and VC, the question I am asked most is how do I get better at raising capital. In chapter 9 I cover the 5 Ps of the Funding Fitness model — a model that will vastly improve your success in raising capital.

FLAWED BUSINESS MODELS

I've referred to the definition of a startup as 'a temporary organ- isation in search of a scalable, repeatable, profitable business model'. Founders often confuse an idea or a product with a business model. It is very easy to fall in love with an idea, and even easier to fall in love with a product. Ideas are cheap and they are everywhere! The idea is the seed that births most startups — and that isn't a bad thing. However, most founders place too much importance on the idea alone. Ideas are interesting, but business models make successful startups. Coming up with a smart idea is easy. Creating a fully blown, viable business model is harder. Most ideas at best identify a market opportunity; and in many cases, even that opportunity needs to be validated.

Business model failures fall into four broad categories:

- *lack of desirability:* This relates to not understanding the problem well enough and/or solving a problem that the target customer does not perceive as relevant.

- *lack of feasibility:* There are many ways a startup can fail to execute. It could be because of poor hiring, focusing on the wrong activities or executing too slowly.

- *lack of viability:* We have talked about default dead or default alive with respect to the critical measures of revenue, growth rates and expenses. Managing cash burn within a business model that ultimately drives to break-even and profitability is essential. There has been a recent dramatic shift in the investor community away from growth startups (companies that focus solely on user growth or other growth metrics — think Twitter) towards yield startups (companies that focus on financial metrics such as break-even and customer acquisition cost — think Google).

- *lack of adaptability:* Startups are by their nature disruptive, but this doesn't mean they can ignore competition. External threats such as government regulation can't be ignored either, especially in highly regulated industries.

There is a huge body of knowledge on how to approach creating your startup. For first-time founders this is often overwhelming or inaccessible. Out of my experiences (both good and bad) in founding, incubating and funding early-stage technology startups, I created the Hollywood Method. This method, discussed in detail in chapter 8, draws on the tools and techniques used in Hollywood to create blockbuster movies.

Myth: You need to be a software developer!

A stereotypical view of a startup founder is of a software developer who eats ramen noodles and sleeps on a friend's sofa. In Australia, my experience is that there are more commercial founders than technical ones. You don't need to be a geek to be successful in a startup, but you need to fill that gap in some way. You need either to have a technical co-founder or to educate yourself enough so you can work with outside technical resources. You don't need to be able to write code.

In fact, sometimes it's a tremendous strength for the driving force behind a startup to be a commercially focused person, rather than someone who is into the code.

That said, you cannot afford to be technically illiterate. You don't need to be able to cut code, but some technical knowledge is essential so you can understand the processes associated with product management and software development. You need to be able to see the reason certain technical decisions are made and what the trade-offs are.

Startups are increasingly outsourcing their software development to third parties — either local or offshore. A lot of these projects end in tears because the product developed doesn't meet the requirements or wasn't what the founder envisioned. Getting into the details of product design, and being able to adequately brief and monitor a third-party development house, will mean you avoid these problems. Though you can be successful and not be a geek, you can't completely ignore the technology.

LEARN FROM HISTORY

From the outset, it's healthy and prudent to consider how you could fail. There are reasons why other people who have gone before you haven't been able to climb the mountain. People who climb Mount Everest look at those who went before them and go, 'Okay, we're going to take this route because those people fell off the cliff going that way, and we're going to use oxygen and Sherpas.' You look at how people have failed before you and learn from them so you can adjust course and not make the same mistakes they made.

The great scientist Isaac Newton said in 1676, 'If I have seen further, it is by standing on the shoulders of giants.' These words ring especially true for startups. As founders, we are always innovating around technology, but often we fail to learn from the mistakes that are made time and time again in our businesses. There is a wealth of data and analysis available about startup failure, yet many founders and early-stage investors don't care to look at it.

DON'T BELIEVE THE MYTHS

A number of myths that surround the startup community compound the already high risk of failure. These myths are perpetuated in popular culture, from movies to the business press. The beliefs and biases that founders bring with them can frequently give them a false idea of what they are getting themselves into. It's important to bust these misconceptions and develop a realistic view of the landscape. In the coming chapters we will discuss the common myths associated with startups and do some serious myth busting. Building a successful startup is hard enough without having a delusional view of what is actually required.

DON'T BE A WANTREPRENEUR

When I take a pitch for a startup, I try to identify as early as possible what the founder's motivation for starting their business is. I try to weed out the *wantrepreneurs* — those who are going into it for the wrong reasons. They are in love with the idea of running a startup, rather than the problem they are solving or the product they are building. They love their idea of the glamour, of being able to tell their friends, 'I'm in a co-working space and I'm working on my startup', but they have no idea how difficult and challenging it's going to be. When the going gets tough, those people fold. They're not committed.

Wantrepreneurs are fuelled by the myths. They have watched *The Social Network*, the movie about Facebook founder Mark Zuckerberg, too many times. It's not about black polo necks and Aeron chairs. It's about solid value propositions and a lot of hard work. Ask any experienced founder if they think running a startup is glamorous and most will laugh in your face.

CASE STUDY: RIGHT SIZING

A few years ago, my incubator took on a promising startup called Sized. The business was looking to solve a common problem facing retail e-commerce businesses — product returns due to incorrect size/fit. When ordering clothing online a lot of purchasers either 'bracket' (purchasing the same item in two different sizes and returning the one that doesn't fit) or take a risk and avail themselves of liberal product return policies. The hypothesis for Sized was that the problem cost online retailers millions and created a poor customer experience. As an idea, this seemed sound.

(continued)

CASE STUDY: RIGHT SIZING *(CONT'D)*

After several weeks of investigating the problem further, the market need wasn't as robust as initially thought. Retailers had factored the costs into their business models, and consumers had developed workarounds and strategies for dealing with the problem. On top of that, we couldn't find a business model that made enough money to justify the investment. It was an excellent idea, with a skilled founder, but ultimately we had to cut it from our portfolio because we couldn't identify a value proposition and business model that worked. Ideas aren't everything. Regardless of how much you are in love with your idea, you need to solve a relevant problem for customers, and the idea must evolve into a scalable business model.

OVER TO YOU
3 STEPS TO MYTH BUSTING

Busting the common startup myths is just as important as understanding the reasons why startups fail. The myths, combined with poor founder behaviours, will accelerate failure. There are a few steps you can take to avoid this.

STEP 1: BE PATIENT

Don't panic! Especially in the early days, you have plenty of time. I am all for the hustle and getting things done. However, one of the best things you can do to improve the success of your startup is to take your time. Don't rush in. It is highly unlikely a competitor will beat you to market.

I meet a lot of founders who are super eager to quit their day job and start working on their startup. I love their enthusiasm, but more often than not I advise against it. If you have a day job, you can work on your startup at night or on the weekends without having to take the risk of losing your regular income. You can use this time to research your target market and customers. You can create and refine your pitch deck. Later in this book, I will teach you how you can cheaply and quickly create wireframes and prototypes of your product so you can test them with your target customers. All of this can be done gradually and with minuscule risk or cost. Being patient means you will have a head-start when you do decide to take the leap and work on your startup full time. It will also mean that you have done your homework and are prepared for your initial product launch and capital raise.

STEP 2: STUDY PEOPLE AND PROBLEMS

Most great founders I know are keen observers of human behaviour. Understanding why people do what they do is an unbelievably useful skill to have as a founder. You need to develop and hone those skills. This is often called ethnographic interviewing or human-centred design. It means watching your target customer in their environment, doing the activity that you want to improve or experiencing the problem you are hoping to solve. This observation, along with asking lots of questions, will give you an increased insight into why your customers do what they do. An even more valuable skill is being able to predict what your customers will do before they do it.

Also start thinking about problems. If you have an idea, think deeply about what problem your idea solves. Is it a big problem? Can the current problem be worked around easily? Are there competitors or other substitutes? Some startups fail because the problem they are trying to solve either isn't considered a significant problem by the customer or isn't perceived as big enough. Finding and solving big, real and hard problems is the key. So get to understand your customers' problems well. Ask them how they have tried in the past to solve those problems and why those solutions didn't work.

STEP 3: JOIN THE COMMUNITY AND GET EDUCATED

One of the wonderful things about founding a startup is that you get to join an amazing, vibrant community, all of whose members are on a similar journey to you. I highly encourage you to seek out and join the startup community in your local area. There will be a host of options available, including founder meetings, hackathons, meet-ups and other events, often hosted by incubators, co-working spaces or VCs. Use these events to connect to other founders and investors. It's important to do this well before you need to raise capital, or even before you have a startup. You never know, you may even meet your co-founder at one of these events.

It is also important to keep up to date on what is happening in the startup ecosystem and to educate yourself in areas such as venture capital, product management, 'tech stacks' and current affairs. Who is doing what in the startup field? A host of websites and printed publications — known as the trade press — will keep you in the loop. That knowledge will be invaluable, informing you of areas that are 'hot' right now, giving you a sense of what other founders are doing. It will also provide you with a bunch of tools and tips you can experiment with.

Your connection with the community, along with a well-rounded education, will help with your first external funding round. This experience is often overwhelming for first-time founders. Who should you approach? Should you raise an angel round first or go straight to a VC? Who are the best angels to work with? What VCs are funding startups in your market segment? How much money should you raise and what is the range of valuations being placed on comparable businesses at your stage? I discuss capital raising in chapter 9. Being connected to the startup community and being across pertinent current news is an excellent way to improve your confidence. There is nothing more helpful than talking to an experienced founder about how to navigate those challenges.

RECAP

The fundamental DNA of a startup has three basic but important strands — the founders, the funding and the business model. The 92 per cent failure rate of startups represents a huge waste, and each strand of that DNA contributes to it.

Founders, funding and flawed business models are what I call the 3 Fs of failure. Being a student of startup failure, learning from history and being realistic will ensure you are better positioned than most founders. You can increase your chances of success by asking yourself the right questions and following a proven methodology.

WHAT'S NEXT

Close your eyes and think of a startup. What comes to mind? What do you believe defines a startup? Is it two guys in a garage? Is it writing lines of code and eating ramen noodles in your parents' basement? Is it people wearing black jeans and polo shirts hammering away on computers?

We know that startups are a hotbed of pressure, passion and emotion. In the next chapter, I'll explain more about why founders fail and why choosing your co-founders can make or break your startup. You'll most likely end up spending more time with your co-founder than with your spouse. So how well do you really know them? How will you both respond when the proverbial hits the fan?

CHAPTER 3
THE FOUNDER MYTH

———

It is almost impossible to separate founders from their startups, since they are practically synonymous. 'Startup founder' conjures up a picture in most people's minds. They are larger-than-life personalities, misfits, rebels. They embody traits that are essential to their success: emotional stamina, a never-say-die attitude. Sometimes these same characteristics limit a founder, and even sink what was an excellent company.

FOUNDER DNA

Startups need founders. They don't need managers or CEOs; those roles are better suited to the corporate world, where the business model has been proven and the company has transitioned to an operational focus. A startup is a transitional entity in search of a scalable, repeatable, profitable business model. It's a journey of enquiry and constant adjustment. And that journey needs a leader — someone with the passion, drive and energy to lead and inspire a team.

Founders are important because they create a shared vision and articulate a clear mission — and they usually embody that vision.

No one will be as passionate or enthusiastic about what a startup is trying to achieve than its founder. A startup is usually birthed by a founder trying to scratch an itch or solve a problem they care about. That is why it is usually a huge mistake for boards and investors to throw out founders. Even though it is a mistake that boards and venture capitalists often make.

Steve Jobs is often quoted as saying, 'Why join the navy if you can be a pirate?' It is that ethos that drives startups to be disruptive and that explains why great founders build amazing cultures. Even as Apple grew, Jobs managed to maintain a startup-like culture by breaking off small teams to work on special projects and giving them a 'sense of startup' even inside a larger organisation.

YOUR OWN WORST ENEMY

Founders are also a paradox. The things that make them a success are often their downfall. Many founders are guilty of self-harm. More than any other factor, it is the founders themselves who determine the success or failure of the venture they found. Or, to put it another way, *founder failure contributes more than any other factor to startup failure.*

Founder failure falls into three broad areas:

1. founder(s) lack capacity.
2. founder(s) lack capability.
3. founder disharmony.

Startups have enough risk in them already without introducing founder risk. That's why sophisticated investors and VCs spend a lot of time getting to know the founders. A founder who is physically and emotionally fit will ensure that ethos of self-care permeates through the whole team — in their relationships with customers, in their dealings with co-workers and in their relationships with investors. Having a founder who is level-headed, self-aware and emotionally intelligent reduces the risk of failure. Conversely, an unpredictable founder will wreak havoc within the company. This is what I mean by founder capacity. It is the fuel that allows a startup to go the distance in their search of a successful business model.

Founder capability is far easier to achieve. There are plenty of books, courses and online resources that can teach a founder the core skills they need to perform effectively. We discuss many of them in this book. Some founders, however, let their ego get in the way; they believe in the myth of the super founder, and they aren't open to learning new skills.

Myth: The Super Founder

The problem with the iconic reputation of many startup founders is that it has perpetuated the stereotype of the 'Super Founder'. There is a belief, in part generated by the mainstream media, that a true startup founder is like a god — all knowing, all seeing, unfaltering, able to leap tall startups in a single bound! I see many first-time founders who fall prey to this myth. But founders, even the great ones, are not gods. Great startup founders are diverse; they come in all shapes and sizes and from all kinds of backgrounds. They surround themselves with great teams and know their limitations. They are constantly trying to improve themselves and their teams, and they tread their own path.

The last big reason why founders fail is as a result of disharmony between founders. Startups are creative endeavours and are often fronted by very passionate leaders. Sometimes this passion generates great outcomes, creating amazing products and businesses, but it can spawn very dysfunctional partnerships, with founders acting like an unhappy married couple rather than business professionals. This is such an important topic that we will discuss choosing and working with co-founders in greater detail later in this chapter.

WHAT MAKES A BAD FOUNDER?

If you have spent any time in the startup community you will have met one. They come in many guises, but they usually succeed in singlehandedly destroying their business from the inside, and a lot of relationships along the way. To a greater or lesser degree, bad founders:

- are arrogant
- demonstrate ignorance
- constantly complain
- blame others
- reject criticism
- listen to the wrong people
- have huge egos
- have an entitlement mentality
- are closed-minded
- create conflict for the wrong reasons
- operate on gut rather than insight or data
- have no hustle (are lazy)
- are susceptible to perception bias (distort the facts to suit themselves)
- refuse or are slow to change their minds
- undervalue their team
- think they have to do it all singlehandedly
- are discriminatory, treating female employees and co-founders with disdain.

The list goes on, but I am sure you get my drift. Bad founders are just plain bad news.

Myth: I need to be CEO

At some point your startup will need full-time attention. That could mean you quit your day job, or you hire someone to run your startup for you, or you rely on a co-founder to perform that role. The best person to run a startup day to day may not necessarily be you. That's where reflecting on your real motivation for starting your company comes in. Do you want to run your business or are you happy to take on another role? It's very important to have a level of self-awareness about what you excel at.

I see a lot of founders forced into leading their startups when in fact they would be much happier just developing the product or leading sales and marketing. Don't feel pressured into becoming the CEO if that's not what you truly want to do. You will end up miserable, and it will reduce your chances of success. Far better to have one of your partners run the company or to hire in an external CEO so you can focus on what you really love doing. While it can be a hard grind, working on your startup should still bring you happiness.

WHAT MAKES A GREAT FOUNDER?

Describing what makes a great founder is much harder than pointing out what makes founders fail. Successful founders are often a contradiction, being able to hold completely opposing positions and demonstrate contrary traits simultaneously. Being persistent and flexible at the same time. Taking risks but also being cautious. Thinking long term, but also solving the problems immediately in front of them. Fail fast, but never give up! This paradox is evident in many great founders. The iconic venture capitalist Marc Andreessen speaks of great founders as having 'strong opinions, loosely held'. Awesome founders have great awareness, resilience and adaptability — and they need it. Elon Musk, the founder of Tesla, likens startups to 'staring into the abyss and eating glass' — staring into the abyss because a single wrong decision by a founder can end the company, and eating glass because you work on the problems the company needs you to work on, rather than the problems you would rather be working on. Great founders therefore usually:

- ▶ walk the talk and are authentic
- ▶ have a bias to action (great hustle)
- ▶ are curious and encourage a learning culture
- ▶ work collaboratively with their teams and stakeholders
- ▶ are people oriented and attract great talent
- ▶ are focused
- ▶ build networks
- ▶ are trustworthy
- ▶ are open to feedback and are 'coachable'
- ▶ learn and adapt quickly
- ▶ work well in ambiguous environments
- ▶ aim to deeply understand the customer (are empathetic).

In my experience, the best founders are also great product people. By that I mean they have great natural skills in understanding customer problems and often have outstanding insight into contrarian solutions to those problems. A disproportionate number of the best founders I know gravitate towards product development rather than sales.

Another observation I will make is that great founders are diverse — they come from all sorts of backgrounds. While progress is being made, we still have work to do in the startup community to encourage and support founders from diverse backgrounds. Bringing a diversity of thinking to the game helps us to be disruptive and solve problems creatively. I strongly believe in the democratisation of entrepreneurship: this should be a field of endeavour that is open to all.

ARE TWO HEADS BETTER THAN ONE?

Founder disharmony — arguments among the founders — is one of the most tragic reasons for startup failure. I have seen it firsthand. Understanding how your personalities complement each other and how they clash is critical. Do you share a common set of values? Are you able to resolve conflicts easily? Is there mutual respect? Knowing yourself and having an open conversation with your co-founders about your strengths and weaknesses at the outset is key.

The people you work with — which includes everyone from co-founders to boards to suppliers and advisers — are as essential to the success of your startup as your business model. You can choose to surround yourself with people who bring value to you as an entrepreneur. They contribute skills that you don't have. They make the journey comfortable, share the load and are dependable in the long run. If you get this wrong, though, it can be unbelievably painful.

Happiness and success are yours if you get it right. You can save yourself time in counselling and spend more time working with people you want to work with. It's not solely about finding people you can have fun with (although that is important). If you get this right, you're going to be more successful, because you will be complementing your strengths and compensating for your weaknesses. Accessing skills you don't have is going to increase your chances of success.

THE HUSTLER, THE HIPSTER AND THE HACKER

There's an interesting convention in the startup ecosystem, which is that every founding team needs a hustler, a hipster and a hacker. The hustler is your sales and marketing focused founder; the hipster is your product design focused founder; and the hacker is your coder. These three founders often divide equity equally between them. You will find many venture capitalists pushing for this triumvirate of co-founders because it is perceived as offering the best combination of skills for success. And that seems great in principle, but in practice managing the different demands and personalities of three co-founders can be a nightmare. It is true that teams of co-founders who complement one another's skills and share the load do have more success, but having multiple founders also adds a great deal of complexity in an already difficult environment.

In many instances, you may not need co-founders. Could you just hire the skills you need? I don't favour one course over the other, but you should certainly deliberate carefully on the question. What magic would a co-founder bring that would justify your giving up equity — a share of your company — in exchange for their involvement? Your equity is your biggest asset; don't give it away on a whim.

I've had the experience of founding companies with four, three and two co-founders, and I've gone it alone. Each experience was completely different, in both positive and negative ways. Each had its benefits. Ultimately it's all about the right people in the right combinations for your business. Just don't rush into teaming up with a co-founder — first do your due diligence.

CASE STUDY: THE VELTEANS

Velteo (from the Greek word meaning improvement) was a startup that built applications on top of the salesforce.com platform and also delivered technical consulting services. I co-founded the business with Con Georgiou, Frank Cuiuli and Patrick Bulacz. Four founders meant there were a lot of 'moving parts'. Getting two people to agree on something is hard; getting four people to agree on anything is nigh on impossible. We were four very different individuals but we had perfectly complementary skills. I had salesforce.com expertise, Patrick was the chief techie, Frank led sales and Con built the culture and drove marketing. Each partner brought something different to the table. Although there was constructive conflict (understatement of the year!), it was one of the tightest, best-built teams I've ever worked with.

We had about 35 employees, and the leadership team and culture was so strong that for the first three years of the business we had zero attrition, meaning no staff left the business. In an early-stage startup that is remarkable. No one left the company because it was such a great working environment, and that was largely due to Con's focus on building the culture and the rest of the leadership team's support of that. We could have different styles but we had common values, which is what held everyone together.

This was a situation in which great co-founders meant the load was shared and the 'whole was greater than the sum of its parts'.

(continued)

> ## CASE STUDY: THE VELTEANS *(CONT'D)*
>
> In 2012 we sold the business for cash to a private equity–backed integrator based in New York who wanted a presence in Australia — a company that was eventually acquired by IBM. They had a number of acquisition choices, but I firmly believe the culture and team we had built were what attracted them. It was a good business, and an excellent example of diversity of people, skills, experience and approach — and healthy conflict — all while maintaining harmony built around a common set of values.

THINK OF THE END BEFORE YOU BEGIN

Due diligence means spending the right amount of time, energy and money on checking out the facts before you act. When I'm working with founders, either as an adviser or as a co-founder, I make it a priority to get to know them both professionally and socially. A business partnership is, as I have suggested, not unlike a marriage. You're going to spend as much or more time with your partners than you do with your spouse. It's important to get this right from the beginning, because it is very hard to unwind these arrangements. Have the difficult conversations early on. Spend serious amounts of time with them before making a decision. Call it a prenuptial agreement, if you like.

What conversations am I taking about? Well, in marriage, it is things like how you are going to resolve conflict and whether you want to have kids. In business, you need to ask many similar questions:

- How are you going to resolve conflicts?
- Can you collaborate well together?

- ► Do you trust your co-founder?
- ► What do you each bring to the table with regard to skills and experience?
- ► How long have you known each other? Do you have history?
- ► Do you like spending social time together?
- ► Do you think you have the same values?
- ► What are your expectations of them, and theirs of you?
- ► What happens in a 'separation'? Do you break the business up, or buy them out, or bring someone else in?

In the end, you and your co-founder(s) are going to go on a fantastic, turbulent journey. The partnership needs to have the strength to survive the ups and downs. You are going to spend a ridiculous amount of time with these people. Listen to your gut. When the going gets tough, will they cut and run or will they stand shoulder to shoulder with you?

CHOOSE YOUR BOARD WISELY

Another aspect of selecting the right people is appointing board members. Most startups look for big names on their boards because they think that will help them raise money or provide them with credibility and kudos. My personal experience is that appointing high-profile directors to your board is disastrous. Sure, you can get such people on your board. You may even find people who know what they're doing! Most of the time, though, the big names won't understand your business, or alternatively they will want to run it. Worst of all is when these high-profile directors don't know your business *and* want to run it. You've got a serious problem when it turns out that instead of having four or five board members, you have four or five would-be CEOs on your board, and they all think they know better than the actual CEO.

This situation leads to disharmony (at best) between board and founders, and creates conflict in the business. I've seen it too many times. When entrepreneurs ask me about boards, my advice is to think carefully about what you want from your board. Is it strategy? Is it governance? Is it an introduction to investors or sales support? Get that clear early and you will conclude that maybe the high-profile names aren't the ones who will give you what you want from the board. Also, remember that your board will change and evolve over time. You will start with a range of skill sets among your board members but over time, as you grow, you will need to change them.

In short, start with an advisory board and try before you buy.

Smaller boards are better than larger boards. For an early-stage startup, if your board is bigger than five you have a problem. Next, ensure your board is an uneven number — boards of three, five or seven members work best. Then ensure you have a diverse mix of skills and backgrounds. You don't want all VCs, or all men, or all entrepreneurs. A great board will be a huge asset to you. Choose it extremely wisely, and ensure they are compensated primarily with stock, not cash — you want them tightly aligned with your success.

Understand the different levels of company structure — ownership vs control. A smart founder is on top of both. Trust me, you can be the majority owner of your company and lose control because of a poorly appointed board.

Lastly, get educated on being a board member yourself and connect with professional institutions. In Australia, the Australian Institute of Company Directors (AICD) Company Directors Course is the best professional education program I have ever done. I cannot recommend it highly enough. Not only will it teach you your responsibilities as a company director, but it will connect you with a network of professionals that will bring value to you for years to come.

AVOID THE SNAKE OIL

A word of advice about advisers! This is something I'm super passionate about, because the startup ecosystem is filled with snake-oil salesmen offering advice for a fee. Lots of people make their living charging startups for services, and some of those services are genuinely helpful and useful. Conversely, there are people who make promises they can't keep and misrepresent themselves: 'Oh yeah, I'll be able to raise you capital. Just give me a retainer.' They don't deliver. Your startup will have scarce resources, so you need to be extra careful about who you engage to work for you. Do background checks. Ask for references and ring them up. Do your due diligence. Ask other entrepreneurs for advice about who is good, who is bad and what experience they've had.

I could tell you horror stories. Not everyone's motives are as honest and straightforward as yours. This is true for advisers, investors and board members. Be careful who you trust. I've seen people invest in a business deliberately to make it fail because they have invested much more in a competing business. I've seen some very unethical behaviour. If it sounds too good to be true, it usually is.

When it comes to investors and advisers, the first money is not usually the best money to take. Waiting for quality people and taking the time to nurture those relationships is always preferable to speed. Again, think about shared risk. Are your advisers prepared to take equity instead of a fee? Even if you don't want to give up equity, the answer to the question will tell you a lot about the motivation of the person or organisation you are dealing with.

OVER TO YOU
3 STEPS TO AVOIDING FOUNDER DIVORCE

STEP 1: GET EVERYTHING IN WRITING EARLY

Document your expectations with your co-founders in an agreement from the start. Even if you're just working on an idea, and before you have formed a business, put agreements in writing. Clarify things such as who's going to do what, how problems will be resolved, what equity people will get for what work, how many hours a week they will work, and whether they will work part time or full time. Ultimately, this will translate into what's called a shareholders agreement, which is a legal memorandum covering what happens, for example, in the event of a break-up of the business partnership. Starting to document those expectations in writing will build a common understanding between you and your co-founders early in the game.

In addition, prepare a founder vesting agreement. This is a document that controls the split of equity between the founders, who essentially 'earn' their equity for delivering to the other partners over time. This avoids the situation where a founder doesn't deliver or leaves a business early. Only founders who deliver and stay the course are rewarded with the full equity percentage agreed at the outset. This is crucial.

STEP 2: TRY-BEFORE-YOU-BUY BOARDS

My advice regarding your board is to go very slowly. Don't appoint a director too early. Start with an advisory board. You will get a feel for people: what they are like to work with, how they react in a crisis and what they want from the experience of working with you. It's a bit of try-before-you-buy. It's equally important to have a board charter, a document that sets out the company's expectations of the board's performance, professionalism, conflicts of interest and time commitment. I've had people sit on my boards, get paid, and turn up to only one or two board meetings a year — if at all. They just think it's a pay cheque. As the entrepreneur, you take the lead. Don't assume that just because these people have been in business for 10 or 15 years they're going to do the right thing, or that they know anything about your particular business. Avoid the pin-stripe suits at all costs.

Articulate what you expect of them and ask what they expect of you. Spell out how much time you need from them, that you expect confidentiality of materials, that they may not invest in things that conflict with your business, or that they disclose their intent to do so before they invest. Start with some form of documentation covering all these areas that can later be turned into a board charter.

In choosing a board, there are ways to find out whether the people you talk to are the real deal. Or maybe they are the real deal but not the right fit for you. Just because we don't choose to marry someone doesn't make them a bad person. In earlier chapters, I've said that you need mentors, people you can call, other entrepreneurs who are further down the track than you who may have connections to the community through which you can do a reference check. The startup community is small, so it's not hard to find someone who knows someone. Do that check — do your due diligence.

You can also ask people directly: 'Why don't you give me three other startups where you've sat on the board so I can call them up and ask them what you're like as a board member?' You can then ask if they show up to board meetings, if they actively take an interest in the company, or just come in to pick up their stock options.

Whether they represent a private or a public company, boards have legal and regulatory obligations. As the founder, and a director of your company, you have legal responsibilities. For example, directors have personal liability when a corporation is trading while insolvent (going broke). These responsibilities are sometimes at odds with the fluid nature of running a startup, but they should be taken seriously. When a company is trading while insolvent — common enough for a tech startup — your personal assets, along with those of all other directors, are on the line. As a result, it can be hard to find someone prepared to sign on formally as company director, and they will expect compensation, insurance and director's deeds to protect them.

STEP 3: SHARED RISK

Steer clear of people (founders, board members or advisers) who are not willing to share the risk. Your partners need to take some of their remuneration in shares or stock options. When they share the same risk of losing money as you, they are more invested in the company's success. When they just want big cash fees and are not willing to take a risk, recognise this as an early warning sign, a red flag. 'Okay, these people aren't prepared to share the risk with me. They're not connected to my journey. They're just looking to make a quick dollar.' Find out what are the usual terms for such deals — the typical proportion of cash to shares — and recruit people who are willing to come along on your journey and share the risk with you. That way you will have a good indicator of people's behaviour and motivations.

Two common deal terms are that either they take some equity instead of part of their fee, or they link their payment to delivering a successful outcome — called a success fee. On the capital-raising front, a VC should not take a fee for investing in your company, but a corporate adviser will charge anywhere from 3 to 6 per cent of the capital raised. If they deliver the capital, and in particular the right capital, it is worth paying the fee. But I would avoid paying a corporate adviser a retainer (a regular monthly fee) on capital raising. Either they get the job done or they don't. If they do, then you pay their success fee — and pay it gladly, as capital raising is a huge drain of time and energy for startups.

For directors, link their fees to stock options. Everyone is aligned. You don't want to be dealing with people who are close to the business but are not aligned with the same risk profile as you.

RECAP

I've made the point that startup failure is largely preventable. Founder risk too is avoidable; this is something you can influence. If you address the issue early by having realistic conversations with yourself and with your stakeholder group, then you can take this risk out of the equation.

As a founder, it is important not to confuse capacity and capability. You need to know the difference and you need to ensure you have both. Be self-aware. Recognising that you can't do it all, that there is no such thing as a 'super founder', is the first step.

Working with the right co-founder can be incredibly rewarding. It brings different skills to the table and makes the whole process more enjoyable. Working with the wrong partner is worse than a double root canal! Best avoid it. Remember that choosing the right business partner is as important as choosing the right problem to solve, so take your time and don't rush into partnerships. Not all people have the same values and approach to business as you, so do your research and choose your business partners carefully.

When you've thought carefully about whether or not you want a partner and about what your strengths and weaknesses are, you can start making choices. If you choose to have a partner, take the time to understand who they are, what values they have, why they want to work with you and how you're going to work together. If you do that, you'll create a functional and productive relationship. You'll both understand what you each bring to the business and will better appreciate each other. As a result, you'll focus on the business and have fun rather than spending time resolving your issues.

WHAT'S NEXT

This may surprise you, but your startup idea is not unique. Ideas are like arseholes — everyone's got one. And it's certainly not the most important element of your startup. In the next chapter, we start a detailed analysis of the reasons why startups fail. Starting with failures relating to ideas and business models, let's understand how to supercharge your startup by turning your bright idea into an even more brilliant business.

CHAPTER 4
IDEAS ARE CHEAP!

Everyone's got one. Founders place enormous importance on their ideas, and I understand their excitement. Every great business starts with an idea. However, excessive faith in ideas is the most common reason for startup failure — a failure that manifests itself in there being *no market need* for your product or service! Founders think their ideas are businesses. Sadly, they're not. Of the 10 reasons for startup failure, four of them relate to idea failure:

- ► solving an irrelevant problem (lack of desirability)
- ► ineffective business model (lack of viability)
- ► poor execution (lack of feasibility)
- ► external threats/competition (lack of adaptability).

I don't want to underplay the power of a great idea. In fact, in this chapter I will talk about ideas I find exciting and why. But I'm going to focus on how to process ideas so they become stronger, smarter and more successful. First, though, the bad news. Everyone has ideas — they are everywhere. Walk into a pub anywhere in Australia and you will be inundated with ideas. It's far easier for people to come up with ideas than it is for them to come up with profitable businesses. Once you understand this point, you have the magic. When you understand the need to have a process to take your ideas through to a solid business proposition, you will stand out from the crowd of wantrepreneurs who bandy about ideas and little else. The difference between successful and unsuccessful founders comes down to this: successful founders turn their great idea into a desirable value proposition and then into a viable business model.

Myth: Ideas are everything

Understanding your value proposition — the problem you are solving, for whom and why — is way more important than your idea. Founders pitch hundreds, if not thousands, of business concepts to me every year. Frankly, I can't even remember them all. It's the great value propositions and corresponding business models that stand out. I bet you have heard someone say about the hugely successful ride-sharing startup Uber, 'Wow! What a great idea. I wish I had thought of that!' In reality, plenty of people had thought of the notion of ride sharing before Uber did. And several startups even got funding. The difference was that Uber had a business model that worked and they executed it relentlessly to win.

If you had to put a rough percentage figure on it, many new founders believe their idea represents more than 95 per cent of the value of their startup, with 5 per cent covering everything else. I would suggest the opposite: the idea represents approximately 5 per cent of the overall value of a startup; 95 per cent of it depends on a great value proposition and business model and a great team executing well.

You can see why some entrepreneurs make this mistake. Look at the language people use. You hear people say of a business such as Facebook, 'That's a terrific idea. I wish I had thought of it.' I want to start to change the way we think about and describe new companies. Uber and Facebook are great businesses that have great business models — they aren't great ideas. Even if you or I had thought of the idea, the real work would have been in executing it. This common misunderstanding sends entrepreneurs onto the wrong path, which is why I feel strongly about it.

Ideas are sparkly. They're inspirational. They are easy to grasp. Ideas are often easier to understand than businesses. Building a brilliant business from the concept is hard work. It is far less glamorous than talking about your idea.

However, we still need the passion that good ideas foster in us to 'fuel' the business. The idea is the juice. The business model is the vehicle. So, let's have a look at how good ideas are born, nurtured and developed to become investable.

IDEAS VS VALUE PROPOSITIONS VS BUSINESS MODELS

Many new founders confuse their idea with a value proposition or a business model, so let's start with some definitions.

An idea can be defined as 'a thought or suggestion around a possible course of action'. The startup community is littered with ideas that were never executed on, or were misconstrued to be a value proposition.

Alex Osterwalder and others, in their excellent book *Value Proposition Design,* define a value proposition as 'the benefits customers can expect from your products or services'. They define a business model as 'the rationale of how an organisation creates, delivers and captures value'.

Essentially, a value proposition describes how you will create value for your customers; a business model describes how you will create value for your business. You need both.

THE FOUR ESSENTIALS OF AN INVESTABLE IDEA

When a founder seeks to pitch a startup to me, my screening and selection process includes evaluating the idea and, more importantly, evaluating the business model (if they have one!). I test for four key components: desirability, viability, feasibility and adaptability.

1. DESIRABILITY: SOLVE A RELEVANT PROBLEM

It may sound crazy, but solve a relevant and important problem for customers and they will beat a path to your door. Of all of the reasons why startups fail, 'no market need' is number one. It doesn't matter how in love with your idea you are, customers need to *care* about your offering, and they will vote with their wallets.

A value proposition is a critical component of the overall business model. It provides the answer to three important questions:

- ► Who are your customers?
- ► What problem are you solving for them?
- ► Why would they value your solution?

These are the components of the value proposition. It's about working out who your customer is, how you are servicing them and what the exchange is. How are you going about that? The value proposition is the core of your business model. It is about determining the fit between your anticipated offering and your customer's needs. If you don't have that value proposition right, then you won't have a strong business model. It's about identifying what that value is. The customer's perception of your value proposition is all that matters. The best value propositions are perceived by the customer as meeting an unsatisfied need. To create a strong value proposition, you need to test it with them — their ruling is final.

Your value proposition must also be substantially better than the status quo. A product that's only incrementally better than what already exists won't fly. Why? The answer is that people are very reluctant to change. They stick with what they know, even if it is disappointing them. Investors also look for a product and value proposition that's going to be disruptive or revolutionary. This kind of approach does one of two things: either it's a vast improvement on what exists today, or it's a disruptive innovation, meaning it challenges what the market already accepts, often taking a contrarian perspective. People who come up with disruptive solutions frame an idea or a problem in a new and different way.

2. VIABILITY: HAVE AN EFFECTIVE BUSINESS MODEL

A business model encompasses the value proposition, the financial mechanism for your business (revenue model, cost structure), your key partnerships, how you get to market (channels), what activities your business performs, and what resources it uses to deliver the product or service.

The best authority on business model development is *Business Model Generation* by Alex Osterwalder and Yves Pigneur. They have developed an excellent tool called the Business Model Canvas, which allows you to develop and explore business models quickly on a single page. It has become the de-facto standard for business model documentation.

Here I'll offer an example that demonstrates all the elements that link the chains of your business and add to the value proposition. Let's look at Google. Google's service allows anyone to use the internet to search for what they want. Google delivers this service free to consumers, monetising those consumer 'eyeballs' by selling advertising products to businesses — known as Google AdWords. This is called a two-sided market. Google delivers a free service to consumers to bring them to Google's platform, then makes money by selling advertising. That's the basis of a business model.

The reason Google succeeds is that it adds more value to everything it does — from how it produces its product, to how it serves its customers and its advertisers, and everything in between. Imagine if a Google search was horribly slow or delivered poor results. What if its ads were too expensive or didn't generate any leads for its advertisers? What Google has achieved is a good idea with a strong business model that is well executed, so it remains the market leader.

There are many different types of business model — from freemium to subscription to fee for service. Regardless of the type, your business model needs to be viable. For me, and most investors, business model viability breaks down into two key factors: *profitability* and *scalability*.

We discuss financial metrics and profitability in chapter 5. Put simply, a profitable business requires that the cost of acquiring customers be less than the value customers bring to your business over their lifetime. Pretty straightforward, when you think about it.

Customer acquisition cost (CAC) is defined as all the costs of acquiring customers over a given period, including all sales and marketing costs, divided by the number of customers acquired. So, if a startup spent $100 000 on sales and marketing (including salaries) over a given period and acquired 100 customers, its CAC would be $1000 per customer.

Customer lifetime value (LTV) is defined as the total value (profit) a customer will deliver to your business over their lifetime less acquisition costs. While there are many highly complex and sophisticated methods of calculating this value, as a rough guide you need to understand (1) how much annual profit (if any) an average customer contributes in a year, (2) what the average customer lifetime is and (3) what your customer acquisition costs are.

Understanding your customer retention rate — that is, how many customers you had last year who are still customers this year — forms the basis for the LTV calculation. If, for example, you had 100 customers last year, only 50 of whom remain customers this year, then your customer retention rate is 50 per cent.

Without getting too geeky, customer lifetime is defined as:

Customer Lifetime = 1/(1 − Customer Retention Rate)

So in the above example the customer lifetime would be two years, calculated as 1/(1 − .50). Now we know how long a customer's lifetime is, we can easily calculate their lifetime value. There are numerous ways to do this, but a quick and dirty calculation is:

Customer Lifetime Value = Annual Profit Per Customer × Customer Lifetime − Acquisition Costs

So if, say, your annual profit per customer was $2000, their lifetime was two years and your acquisition costs were $1000, then:

Customer Lifetime Value = ($2000 × 2 − $1000) = $3000

Why does all this matter when designing a business model? Well, for a business model to be viable the ratio between lifetime value (LTV) and customer acquisition cost (CAC) is very important. Firstly, the lifetime value of customers needs to be higher than the acquisition cost. How much higher? Viable business models typically show LTV at three to five times higher than CAC. In addition, it is good practice to recover your customer acquisition costs in the first year. I meet many founders who have not considered the real costs of customer acquisition, and think that 'the web' is a cheap way to acquire customers. That isn't necessarily true.

As well as being *profitable*, effective business models also need to be *scalable*. Scalability is a term that gets thrown around a lot in relation to tech startups, but what does it really mean? A scalable business model is one that can *dramatically increase revenues without an associated or equivalent increase in costs*. A software business is typically scalable, as once the initial software development costs are incurred, additional revenue (sales) can be generated with a limited increase in cost. A services business, however, is usually not scalable, as in order to deliver additional revenue you usually need to hire more people.

Areas of your business model that you can explore for scalability include:

- *channels:* Can you use different channels?
- *partnerships:* How can you leverage partners for scale?
- *infrastructure:* Do your systems and processes help you to scale?

Investors will look for scalability in your business model. Use market testing to prove out aspects of scalability early.

3. FEASIBILITY: HAVE THE RESOURCES TO GET THE JOB DONE

Much is made of having the right team in your startup, and with good reason. Even if you have identified a desirable value proposition and have built a viable business model, you still need resources to execute. And execution is critical to any startup. Resources fall into a number of categories, including:

- human (your team)
- financial (your funding)
- physical (plant and equipment)
- intellectual (brands, patents)
- partnerships.

Of all these resources, the most critical to execution are your human resources — your team. I have seen many great startups fail through a lack of the right resources. For example, given that their initial teams are usually quite small, the impact of a single bad hire can be disastrous. So I counsel founders to take their time with early hiring, even if it means some short-term pain. It's important to build a team to complement you and your style. Hiring a diverse team of professionals who augment your strengths and offset your weaknesses, and who you get on well with, makes the journey so much easier. Regardless of how talented an individual is, if they don't fit with your working style or your company culture then it's not worth hiring them. You will spend more time managing the relationship than managing the business. As a startup, you can't afford that time and energy.

In addition, does your team have the right skills to do the job? It is critical that your team has a skill balance and, most importantly, that you have the leadership skills to direct the team. For me, this is where founder fitness comes in: having the physical, mental and emotional capacity to go the distance. We discuss founder fitness in chapter 6.

Ultimately, execution is about the *right people doing the right things*. As a founder, you are responsible for both hiring and attracting the right people, then leading them and focusing them on the right activities.

4. ADAPTABILITY: MANAGE EXTERNAL THREATS

At times it may seem like your startup is the centre of the universe — it isn't. I spoke at the beginning of the book about how often startup failure is misunderstood as an external event. Just to remind you, startup failure is usually caused by 'internal' events — that is, events that are well within the founder's control and that, if they know and learn about them, can be avoided. This isn't always the case, however, and it is important to keep an eye on the external environment, the context in which your startup operates. Examples of external threats include:

▸ being outcompeted by a competitor with a substitute product

▸ a change in the regulatory environment in your industry

- ▶ a change in social attitudes

- ▶ a change in capital markets that dries up funding

- ▶ invention of a disruptive technology

- ▶ a competitor increasing customer switching costs.

Being outcompeted can be both an external and an internal threat. The startup ecosystem is littered with the metaphorical bodies of companies that had great products but didn't get traction. The best product doesn't always win. Suppose you have established that there's a need for your product, you have developed a business model and have a great product, but your go-to-market strategy is weak. You haven't considered the competitive landscape. That's an internal event. It could be that you and your team have become arrogant and don't take heed of what is happening in the competitive landscape.

There are many examples of that in tech. Having a need, a business model and a great product are essential, but you must also have a good strategy around sales, marketing, consumer awareness, timing and distribution. All these things will affect your success. Don't obsess over your competitors early, but definitely keep them in the frame when you are considering your business model and the attractiveness of your market.

PUTTING IT INTO PRACTICE: CATAGRAM—INSTAGRAM FOR CATS

Many a great-sounding idea never evolves into a great business. Imagine a potential founder: 'I've got this great idea: Instagram for cats!' The first quality that I look for in the idea, that kernel of a potential business, is whether it meets a market need. Now, cat owners are strange people. They send their cats postcards when they go on holidays. That's true—I read it on the web! So perhaps there is a need for a Moggie Instagram. I'm never going to dismiss an idea just because it seems ridiculous. I'll start by asking the entrepreneur what evidence they can show me that cat owners are hanging out for a Catagram. Here are some things I might ask or do to investigate the market need:

- ▶ How many cat owners are there?

- ▶ What is the average number of cats per owner?

- ▶ How many cat pictures are currently being posted on existing platforms?

- ▶ Conduct a survey of cat-posting Instagram users to see what they need.

- ▶ Why do they post pictures of their cats?

- ▶ Has anyone else tried this? Did they succeed or fail?

The list of questions and research topics is endless. Not all cat owners are the same. Not all of them take photos of their cats. Of those who do take kitty snaps, some can't even turn on a computer. They are happy to print their kitty pics down at the department store and create a cat album and put it on their bookshelf. Of the digitally savvy cat owners, many will post them on Facebook. Then there are those cat owners who post on Instagram. Are they the market? Maybe not. Perhaps they are happy with Instagram. So who is the group of cat owners that want this product? It's not just any cat owner; it's computer-savvy cat owners who take photos of their pets, and are unhappy with their experience using Instagram and Facebook.

Okay, now we're getting somewhere. But wait! The next question is the big one: will someone see enough value in Catagram to pay for it? Huh? Instagram is free. Facebook is free. Why would cat owners pay to post their pics? I'm not saying they wouldn't pay. I'm just asking why they would pay. To get someone to pay for anything involves a value proposition. We pay money for stuff we value — it's as simple as that. If your idea can't be transformed into a value proposition and then into a business model, you don't have a business. Ask yourself, are you solving a relevant problem, and can you build a viable business model? (Oh, and if you think of a viable business model for Catagram, email me. ;-)

Myth: Secrecy is key

I am often asked by founders to sign a non-disclosure agreement (NDA) before they will discuss their startup with me. This is usually a huge red flag. Secrecy is not a business model. An idea that needs to be kept secret is usually weak. It is highly unlikely that your idea will be copied. If you are worried about someone stealing and copying it, that says a lot about the strength of your team, your business model and your experience. Ideas are easy. Executing on them is much harder. It is very rare that you need to keep your idea or startup a secret.

OVER TO YOU
3 STEPS TO A BETTER IDEA

STEP 1: FIND A PROBLEM YOU CARE ABOUT

Look for problems in the marketplace that you care about and can solve. Who likes putting in their own petrol? No one, but we will do so to keep down the price of filling our tank. Could you solve that problem? Who wants to go to the supermarket? Could drones be the answer? Crowded trams, expensive housing, clogged roads, rude people in queues, ineffective leaders, boring commutes, divorce, unhappiness, poverty, dirty water — the world is full of problems for you to solve. Find a problem that you are passionate about. The best ideas I have seen have come from a founder with 'an itch to scratch'. A founder who cares deeply about the problem is going to stay the course when things get challenging and is more likely to bring unique insight to the problem.

STEP 2: EXPERIMENT WITH VALUE PROPOSITIONS

What is your value proposition? What problem are you solving, and who are you solving it for? Is the problem perceived by the customer to be important enough? How much value will they place on your solution? Spend a lot of time here and explore the options. Once you've identified your prospective customers, go out and observe them. Observation is a skill we will talk more about in later chapters, but I cannot emphasise enough how important it is when developing a potential value proposition.

Ask potential customers a lot of questions about the problem: How do they solve it today? Do they work around it? Do they ignore it? Is there a competitor out there that's already solving the problem for them more quickly or more effectively than you can? Then ask yourself, what is the value to my customers of having that problem solved? People will pay a lot for what makes them happy or saves them money, for example. What gains are you delivering and what pains are you relieving? Customers don't pay for stuff that adds complexity to their lives or confuses them. They might not even pay for your product if another product — even one that is more expensive — gives them status or makes them look or feel successful or glamorous. Be sure to explore both the spoken and unspoken needs of the potential customer. Remember, successful value propositions are desirable in the customer's eye.

STEP 3: EXPERIMENT WITH BUSINESS MODELS

You know all about the problem you're solving, why it's a big problem and how people solve that problem today. You know who the customer is, and what your value proposition for them is. Now you are ready to create your business model, to explore alternatives and to conduct research to back it up.

There are great tools and techniques for developing business models. As I mentioned earlier, the de facto standard for business model development is the Business Model Canvas, which is described in Osterwalder and Pigneur's *Business Model Generation*.

The Business Model Canvas allows you to outline all the key elements of your business model on a single page, including channels, customer segments, revenue streams, costs, partnerships, customer relationships and the value proposition. It is an easy process to follow and is becoming the standard means of communicating business models between investors and startups. It will also help you communicate your business model to your team. Of course, having your team and your investors understand all the aspects of your business model is essential.

In addition, it will help you to explore variations of a business model. You might have three or four different options. Do you charge a subscription price? Do you go for a 'freemium' model ('I'll give you a little for free, then I'll charge you')? Do you charge an annual fee? Do you charge a one-off fee? Looking at those possible variations of your business model will help you to explore different combinations. You can then test these different business models to determine which one best matches your business.

CASE STUDY: FOXTEL VS STREAMING (BUSINESS MODEL DISRUPTION)

As an example of how a business model can be disrupted, look at Foxtel, the cable TV provider in Australia. Foxtel had substantial set-up costs, having to deploy a vast cable infrastructure and to purchase expensive content to provide to subscribers. However, after many years of being the only game in town, Foxtel is now facing substantial competition from new market entrants such as Netflix and Stan. These new competitors stream their video content on demand and have no advertising, meaning consumers can watch what they want, when they want. As streaming services are delivered over existing internet infrastructure, the set-up costs for these services are lower. As a result, Foxtel have had to lower their subscription price, and are trying to introduce their own streaming products.

In this case, you've got two competing business models: Foxtel is trying to make money out of subscribers, but their customers are frustrated because they still have to wade through many ads. Customers pay a large subscription, but Foxtel is still trying to make money out of advertising revenue. Plus, they're telling me what I can watch and when I can watch it. So along comes Netflix, which still demands a subscription, but I've got no ads, and I can consume it where and when I choose.

The superior business model wins the day.

RECAP

Ideas are cheap and they are everywhere. Having an attractive idea doesn't mean you'll have a great company. The key to having a successful startup is turning your fantastic idea into a business with products or services that people will pay for. That means developing a compelling value proposition, and embedding that value proposition in a viable business model. Although there is plenty of work to turning an idea into a business, deeply empathising with your potential customers will give you valuable insight into the best way to solve their problems.

The four critical elements of an investable idea are:

▶ desirability (solving a relevant problem for a customer)

▶ viability (developing a business model that works)

▶ feasibility (having the right team doing the right things)

▶ adaptability (keeping an eye on the external environment).

Life is different for founders who understand these four critical elements. You know the market you're serving. You understand the problem you're solving deeply, better than anyone else. And you know the people whose problem you are solving. That gives you a level of confidence that your business model is going to work and that customers will pay for your product. In fact, you don't even have to convince them that your product solves their problem. They'll know that straightaway, and they'll beat a path to your door.

WHAT'S NEXT?

Show me the money! In the next chapter, I explain why funding is the oxygen of your startup. You need the right amount. Not enough and you suffocate; too much and you pass out. Do you know how much money your startup needs? Can you take too much money? How can you avoid running out of cash?

CHAPTER 5
CASH IS KING

Cash is king when it comes to startups. It is the oxygen that keeps your business alive. When founders think about cash, they typically focus on fundraising, which is important, but not the *most* important financial aspect that founders should consider. Of the 10 main reasons why startups fail, three can be attributed to funding-related issues:

- ▶ running out of cash
- ▶ being overfunded
- ▶ investor disharmony.

It might surprise you to know that startups can be both overfunded and underfunded, which is entirely at odds with what most people believe. Most entrepreneurs will recognise the problem of being underfunded. Many are less aware of the risks of being overfunded. Both problems can sink a business. Here I'll explain just how each of these funding situations can lead to failure and how the investment-ready founder can prepare for them. Finally, the relationship you have with your investors is also extremely important. If you don't get this right, then investors can make your life as a startup founder a living hell.

Myth: Fundraising equals success

In their early stages, most startups live from one funding round to the next. Founders are often fixated by capital raising. It's understandable, since without capital most startups wouldn't survive. However, because they live in a capital-starved environment, when they do get funded many startups think they have made it to the finish line. In fact, fundraising is just the beginning. Having the right mindset is saying, 'Yes, let's work hard to get our funding, but now we have it, the real challenge begins!' You have to deploy your funding in the most efficient way. The capital is finite, so it's essential to focus on using it appropriately and not to call the war won when you get money in the bank account. Equating fundraising success with business success is a mistake many founders make, and the financial media perpetuate this myth. Significant capital raisings are sexy, and they make good copy, but getting your first customer, sending out your first invoice or your shipping your first products are far more important milestones. Admittedly, you can't achieve those goals without fundraising, but don't take your eye off the main game. Funding is merely the fuel to help you build a sustainable business.

In the previous chapters, failures related to the idea and failures related to founders are discussed. Most startup failures fall into one or both of these categories. Whatever the underlying causes, however, the main outward indicator will be that the startup runs out of money. This generally occurs because the startup (for a variety of reasons) burns through its available cash and fails to secure any further funding, usually because investors no longer believe in the business or the people running it.

REALITY CHECK: FINANCIALS MATTER

There is no sugar-coating it: if you are a startup founder you need to be intimately across the financial model and performance of your business. If the thought of accounting causes you to break out in a sweat, then it's time to tackle that fear. You cannot start and run a business without a good grasp of how it makes money.

On the bright side, you don't have to do it alone. You need a bookkeeper from day one. You need someone who is going to be responsible for the finances of the business. When you can afford it, a great finance director or CFO is invaluable. But they are only there to support you. It's crucial that you, as a founder, understand how the business operates at an economic level.

For founders, it's easy to ignore the financials and focus on other metrics, such as user growth. Another myth is that startups don't need to be profitable. This is patently untrue, and the sooner founders recognise they need to build sustainable businesses the better. However, finding and building sustainable economic models is hard. Most people want to take that easy route and ignore the underlying financial model of their business.

WHY IS IT IMPORTANT?

You need an understanding of what makes your startup tick financially. For example, how much money do you have? How long will it last? (Understanding these two points alone is a vital first step.) How do you make money? When will you become profitable and no longer need external funding?

You're going to be asked these questions by potential investors, and by potential employees who want to understand if your business is sustainable and whether they should invest their time or money in it.

Financial awareness and acumen are more important than ever because there has been a shift in the venture community away from pure growth companies towards profitability and yield.

Historically, venture capitalists were far more willing to invest — to be bullish, in the investment community parlance — in companies that had plenty of growth potential but weren't profitable. Some didn't even have a plan or path to profitability. It was as though the investors and founders had agreed, 'Well, we will just work out how we're going to make money from the business later, but for now we are just going to grow users or usage.' Many iconic tech companies were funded, and continue to be funded, on that premise. Recently, however, there has been a dramatic shift away from that approach, and now the venture community wants profitable companies or at least companies that have a strong and clear path to profitability.

It's understandable that founders are a bit confused. You've got these businesses that are colossal and well regarded in the technology community, but they don't make profits. Those days are over, however. Investors now expect startups to have a sustainable economic model. Although the conventional wisdom says you can make profits just by creating a fast-growing user base, investors are shying away from that model, and rightly so. Investors now say, 'It's great that your user base is growing, but how are you going to make money? We are not going to fund this business forever.'

For founders, it's easy to ignore the financials and focus on other metrics such as user growth. It's ingrained in the mythology of startups that they don't need to be profitable. Finding and building a sustainable economic model is much more complicated than it looks. Most people want to take the easy route.

I sometimes come across founders, especially in the early stages of growth, who don't have the knowledge or the skills to understand the financial aspects of their business. They are either commercially focused, with all their effort devoted to sales, or technology focused, putting all their effort into the product. I don't come across many with an operational focus whose attention is fixed mainly on cash flow, break-even points and unit economics. Founders need to take personal responsibility for the financial aspects of their business. Sure, go and outsource administrative aspects such as invoicing or tax compliance if you want, but you still need a deep understanding of the economics of your business to survive.

BUILDING A FINANCIAL MODEL

At its simplest, the aim of any business is to make money and be sustainable. Developing a financial model is the first step to understanding the economics of your business. You should start on your financial model as early as possible. Even when evaluating different go-to-market strategies, it's useful to model the financial impact of those different options — for example, charging a monthly subscription vs a per-use pricing model.

Don't be afraid of this step. There are plenty of tools and resources available to help you fast-track the development of your financial model. At a basic level, a financial model should show:

- ▶ a projection of your revenues
- ▶ a projection of your costs
- ▶ a projection of your profitability
- ▶ a projection of your cash inflows and outflows
- ▶ the assumptions used to develop the model.

There is an adage in the venture community that goes, 'The thing that is always right about early-stage financial models is that they are always wrong.' When you're preparing early-stage financial models, it's best to model a maximum of 12 to 24 months ahead. Trying to predict and model years three, four and five is like reading tea leaves.

I haven't seen a startup financial model that has been delivered with 100 per cent accuracy, ever. At best, they're educated guesses. In the early stage of a business, you just don't have the historical data to help you predict what it's going to look like in the future. As a business gets older, there's more data and more history from which to create a more accurate forecast.

CASE STUDY: WHEN $8M IS NOT ENOUGH

One business, REFFIND, provides an interesting case study in relation to funding. It's a company I founded in 2014 and listed on the Australian Stock Exchange in 2015. The company raised $8 million as part of an initial public offering (IPO). However, during the capital-raising process potential investors had offered us much more money — up to $50 million — in what is called an oversubscribed funding round. Everyone in the business team thought that A$8 million was enough money for us to reach break-even (when income matches expenses) and to become profitable in the time we had allowed. As it turned out, our revenue was slower to realise than we had expected, which meant we burned more cash than expected. We had to go out and raise additional capital. As a result, the stock market — our shareholders — punished us by driving down the stock price.

STARTUP CASH: ARE YOU DEFAULT DEAD OR DEFAULT ALIVE?

In chapter 1, I introduced the terms *default dead* and *default alive* as coined by investor Paul Graham. In short, your startup is either burning money to a point where it will need another funding round, if it can get one (default dead), or it's burning money but revenue is growing fast enough that the business will break even before the money runs out (default alive).

Startup cash economics are pretty easy to understand if you break them down to their simplest form. In short, cash is king. There are four key aspects you need to understand when it comes to cash:

- ► How much cash do you have?
- ► How much cash do you need?
- ► How fast are you burning cash?
- ► When will you run out of cash?

HOW MUCH CASH DO YOU HAVE AND HOW MUCH DO YOU NEED?

Your initial financial model will give you an indication of how much money you are going to need. My view on this is you will need 50 to 100 per cent more money than you think you will. Why? Because your initial financial model is a best guess. You have made educated assumptions, but those assumptions have not been tested in the real world. When you're going into your initial funding discussions, it's much better to be asking for more cash than you think you need so you have a buffer.

There is another reason why startup founders don't ask for more funding initially: fear of dilution. Dilution is the reduction of a founder's ownership stake in the business as a result of outside investors injecting money into the company. It is a function of the value being placed on the business, divided by how much money is going in. For example, if a startup is valued at $1 million prior to the investment (called a pre-money valuation) and an outside investor puts in $200 000, then this will reduce the founder's stake by approximately 16.6 per cent. This is calculated by dividing the investment, $200 000, by the new post-investment valuation (called a post-money valuation) of $1 200 000.

Startup founders who fear dilution often underfund their businesses to maintain a larger ownership percentage. My strong advice is, don't do it! Yes, you will be giving up more of your business by injecting more capital into it. But if you use that money appropriately, it's going to grow faster and give you a greater chance of success. By taking on enough capital, even though that means giving up some equity, you can expect a slice of a much larger pie in the future. The funding environment can and does change. Money in the bank now buys you time and gives you some certainty of survival in the near term. Remember, 92 out of 100 startups fail. We're trying to reduce that failure rate and increase the 8 per cent success rate, so make sure your business doesn't fail because it's underfunded.

HOW FAST ARE YOU BURNING CASH AND WHEN WILL YOU RUN OUT?

How fast your startup is using cash, known as the *cash burn rate*, is usually calculated as a monthly figure. In essence, it represents monthly cash flows into your account minus monthly cash flows out of your account. For most startups, it's a negative number. One source of confusion for founders is the difference between a profit and loss accounting report (P&L) and the actual cash flows in a business. Often a startup may be profitable on a profit and loss basis, meaning revenues are larger than expenses, but due to poor cash flow management — for example, paying out cash (trade creditors) faster than taking in cash (trade receivables) — the business may still run out of cash. Managing your cash should be a top financial priority for a founder. Knowing your monthly cash burn is the starting point. If you don't know this number off the top of your head, you aren't managing your startup appropriately.

The last component is understanding when you will run out of cash. Hopefully that is later rather than sooner. Calculating the time you have remaining, referred to as your *cash runway*, is pretty easy. You take your monthly cash burn and divide it by the amount of cash on hand. That will give you a rough guide to how many months of life your startup has left. You can then factor in current revenues and monthly revenue growth. How much extra time does this revenue buy you? If your revenue and its growth gets you to break-even and a cash flow positive position before the money runs out, then happy days — you are in a default alive position, which is a great place to be for any startup, because it gives you the breathing space to raise additional capital on your terms and to focus on more than just survival.

OVERFUNDING: GIVING THE STARVING MAN A FEAST

Overfunding a startup is equivalent to giving a starving man a feast. In the early stages, it usually doesn't have much money to work with, so the founders are operating on low or no income. They're in very humble offices or no offices at all. They're running extremely lean. You would think that giving them money would necessarily be a good thing, but this is not always the case. Giving too much money, in a lump sum, to a startup that has experienced a very lean cash environment raises a couple of risks: they can become complacent or wasteful, or both.

Complacency is the death knell of a startup. I have seen founders who are so relieved by a sudden influx of money that they take their foot off the accelerator and relax. Now they have 12 to 18 months' worth of cash, they take things a little bit easier. This is often a reflection of the maturity and experience of the founding team, and can be allowed to happen by boards that don't manage their founders well enough. That's the best-case scenario.

The worst-case scenario is that they become wasteful. They're sitting on a huge pile of cash. They buy luxury cars and throw big launch parties. They move into palatial offices filled with plush furniture and big murals on the walls. Look for the Aeron chairs — I tell you, they're a sure sign of an overfunded startup!

If you've seen the HBO startup comedy *Silicon Valley*, you'll know what I mean. That show hits close to home sometimes — it's funny because it's true. In one episode, Bachmanity Capital win a huge amount of funding, and the first thing they do is throw a massive party on Alcatraz and blow it all. When I see extravagant parties and fancy furniture and binge spending, it tells me the startup is overfunded. That sort of wastefulness and recklessness means investors are going to lose their money. So how do you avoid that? Funding tranches.

Funding tranches can be a win–win scenario for both the investor and the founder. Funding in tranches means an investor commits to a line of funding but provides the cash only once certain performance milestones are achieved. For example, an investor might say, 'Okay, I'm going to provide you with $2 million, but I'm going to give it to you in $500 000 increments, based on your achieving certain mutually agreed measures of success.'

This approach provides two benefits. The first is that it reduces the risk to the investor, avoiding a situation where they transfer a large sum into the startup's bank account and just hold their breath and hope for the best, placing themselves at the mercy of the founders.

The second benefit is to the founder. Now, most founders seek as much funding as possible, and they want the security of knowing that the funding is committed. In this scenario they know that so long as they achieve certain milestones the investor is committed (possibly through an escrow arrangement) to providing the agreed funding for the business. It keeps the founder focused and the investor protected. The investor's risk is reduced, and the startup is committed to delivering, which balances out the needs of each party.

Good funding is always hard to come by, so founders who are open to tranche-based funding will have a better chance of securing it. It's a mature and realistic approach, with funding tranches released by certain triggers, such as reaching user growth or revenue milestones, or meeting agreed product feature set goals. The important thing to understand is that most investors don't want businesses to fail. They will continue to fund a business if it's making progress. It's unrealistic to expect them to throw good money after bad. If a startup isn't hitting the milestones they said they were going to, that's a clear red flag for investors. Founders need to understand that in a capital-scarce environment, investors are going to ask for these types of conditions.

MANAGING FOUNDER/ INVESTOR HARMONY

Just as disharmony between co-founders leads to startup divorce and failure, disharmony between founders and their investors can easily destroy a startup and the reputations of the founders involved. Once the money is in the bank, founders can often take investors for granted. This is a mistake. Not only will you likely need your investors in future funding rounds of your existing startup, but you will also want to develop a relationship of trust with your investors for any future venture. Successful founders who have treated their previous investors well find it much easier to raise capital a second, third or fourth time.

The first step in managing your investors is to set and understand their expectations. Here are some questions to consider:

- ▶ What level of involvement are they expecting in the business?
- ▶ How and when do they expect to be communicated with?
- ▶ What time frames are they thinking of in terms of capital return (exit)?
- ▶ What are their attitudes to risk and reward?
- ▶ What expectations do they have for founder salaries?
- ▶ What are their views about you taking money off the table?

You need to ensure your investors really understand your business. I have seen countless investors fund a business they did not understand, only to turn around and criticise the founders for their approach or underperformance. Make sure every single one of your investors understands your business model and the business plan for the next 12 months. Use your Business Model Canvas to walk your investors through the key aspects of your value proposition and business model. What are the key proof points and milestones you are looking to achieve to indicate you are on track? How and when will you measure and report on those key metrics?

Be transparent with your investors. Set up regular formal and informal communication points — perhaps a monthly or quarterly investor pack highlighting the key financial and operational aspects of the business. Be forthright in your communications around cash burn and cash runway. It's important they are clear about that. You may be coming back to them for more funding. They should not be surprised if the business is approaching the point where it runs out of cash. I find a monthly or quarterly coffee catchup with your biggest investors is also beneficial in communicating the nuances of what you are seeing in the market. They can help you, and they will appreciate your being open and transparent with them.

If your business is not hitting milestones or is underperforming against plan, then this is not the time to avoid your investors. In fact, this is the time to overcommunicate with them. A lack of information is a surefire way to get your investors offside. Be honest and transparent — in good times and in bad. If you chose your investors wisely at the outset, have connected them to the business plan and have communicated well, then they should be understanding when things go wrong.

OVER TO YOU
3 STEPS TO AVOID FUNDING FAILURES

STEP 1: DO A REALITY CHECK

One factor that amplifies funding-related failures more than most is that founders lie to themselves. They are optimists, and often they need to be. When it comes to the financial and funding aspects of a startup, however, this optimism can be self-sabotaging. Your financial and cash models will have been built on a number of assumptions. Are those assumptions being proven true or false every month by the real data? Are you seeing what you want to see? There is no point in creating a reality distortion field. I have seen founders ignore the facts for months because they weren't convenient or they were hanging on to the hope that something would change. The data is the data. Sometimes you just have to call bullshit on yourself and adjust your plan.

I suggest reviewing your initial 12-month financial model and identifying all of the assumptions you made, for example on pricing, the average sale size, the average cost of hiring a developer or estimated marketing costs. Now, what does the reality teach you about those assumptions? Were you right or wrong, or is the jury still out? Do you need to change course? Do you need to slow down or speed up hiring? Do you need to look at your pricing model? This will be different in each case. Whatever your particular situation, there is no point in ignoring the inconvenient truths — get out in front of them now and do something about them.

STEP 2: DETERMINE IF YOU ARE DEFAULT DEAD OR DEFAULT ALIVE

I've said it before and I'll say it again: you need to be on top of the cash in your startup more than any other resource. It is your oxygen. You should be able to quote your cash burn and runway numbers off the top of your head, and understand the impact every decision you make has on that runway. Want to hire a more senior developer than you originally planned (expense)? Cool, how much runway does that eat up versus the benefit it delivers? I'm not saying don't make the hire, I'm saying you need to understand that decision will have an impact on your startup's lifespan. You will be constantly trading off time (cash) for outcomes. Framing decisions that way can be liberating. It allows you to cut through the noise and get to the essence of a decision. You are essentially on a burning platform. Reid Hoffman, the founder of LinkedIn, likens starting a company to jumping off a cliff and building a plane on the way down. It's a beautiful metaphor. Knowing if you are default alive or default dead will focus you and your team. It's not about creating a sense of fear or dread; it's about approaching the problem realistically. All businesses ultimately need to generate or raise cash to survive.

STEP 3: CREATE A DASHBOARD OF THE METRICS THAT MATTER

Leading a startup is a challenge. You have to get on top of all aspects of finding a sustainable, scalable, profitable business model; attracting and retaining talent; building a product that customers will love and pay for; and managing the cash. There are so many things to consider that it is often overwhelming for founders.

To make things easier, create a dashboard of the three to seven metrics that matter most for your startup. Ignore the rest for now. Although it will be different for every startup, the most common metrics will relate to the categories of finance (cash burn, runway), product (user growth, daily active users) and sales (average customer acquisition cost, average revenue per customer, new customers added). You get my drift.

Select the key metrics that matter for your business. Publish them often and visibly to your team, your board and your investors. Live and die by them. Put them on a large monitor in your office or a whiteboard. It doesn't matter how you communicate them; just make them visible and make them important. Use them to drive the agenda of your team meetings. Don't get carried away. Just choose the ones that matter now, the metrics that will influence your success or failure. Use this as a rallying point. It will help you focus, prioritise *and* communicate.

RECAP

Cash is king in startups. If you run out of money you'll go out of business, it's as simple as that. There are three drivers to funding-related failures:

- ▶ underfunding
- ▶ overfunding
- ▶ arguments with your investors.

Keep a firm handle on all three. Know your current cash status. Is your startup default dead or default alive? Do you have enough cash in the business to continue? Be a financially educated and savvy founder. Understanding the financial aspects of your business is a critical skill for a founder. Knowing the financial model of your business is just as important as knowing your product offering. Don't bullshit yourself. Startups that ignore this frequently burn through their cash and go out of business. There's not an endless supply of capital for businesses, and your purpose is to make a profit and be sustainable. Stay lean — and stay away from expensive office fit-outs and company cars.

Investors beat a path to the door of profitable startups. Once you are default alive, having achieved cash flow break-even, you'll be able to self-fund. This shifts the power balance between investor and founder, meaning you'll be in the driver's seat. You'll now be far better placed to dictate investment terms, and you'll achieve a much better valuation for your business.

Your startup is going to live! This is an amazing moment for you as a founder, and you will have become a member of a very small club. Now you can focus on the business and not on capital-raising. This is way more fun for founders.

WHAT'S NEXT

In the next chapter, we will look at the traits that make a fit founder. The ancient Greek aphorism 'Know thyself' is especially applicable to startup founders today. Startups are a full-contact sport. They are physically, emotionally and mentally taxing. How well do you know yourself and how you will react in a combat zone?

CHAPTER 6
FOUNDER FITNESS

On 9 July 2015, I listed my first company on the Australian Stock Exchange (ASX). REFFIND, a human resources technology company, allowed businesses to better communicate with their employees. It had a web portal for company content and a mobile application for employees to use. I had founded the company in 2014 and had good early success with some high-profile customers.

At the time, some great technology companies listed on the ASX, so we decided to list our business through an Initial Public Offering (IPO). The next four months are a blur. I spent weeks travelling between Sydney, Melbourne, Hong Kong and Singapore briefing institutional investors on the IPO. I was packing in eight to ten meetings a day, not to mention countless lunches, dinners and drinks. To add to the load, I had to step in as interim CEO just before listing. On the day of listing, I weighed 120 kilos, felt like shit and was completely exhausted. Then the hard work began!

The IPO was a success: we raised the capital easily and were many times oversubscribed, meaning there was far more demand than stock available. In fact, we had more than $50 million in demand and only $8 million of stock available.

The stock performed well at first, but investors then sold off hard. Over the course of the 30 weeks following listing, our stock price went from 20c to almost $2 (reaching almost $200 million in market capitalisation) and back again. It was the worst time of my professional career. As the saying goes, 'Success has many fathers; failure is an orphan.' We went from being a darling to a dog. And with that went a lot of things that I hadn't expected and certainly wasn't prepared for.

Firstly, I wasn't in good physical shape to deal with the stress. And stress there certainly was. Angry calls from investors, tough questions from the board and an increasingly hostile business press. And then there were the internet trolls — 'heroes' on discussion boards who are the best armchair generals in existence. I was spending more and more time in damage control, and less and less in managing the business. It had a huge personal impact on me.

It started with sleepless nights. I couldn't switch my mind off, constantly turning over what I should be doing. I was getting maybe two or three hours' sleep a night then getting up and working a 12- to 14-hour day. I became increasingly frustrated and angry at work and at home. Then came the death threats from nutcase investors. When your family is threatened, it puts things into perspective.

Things got progressively worse, and I started thinking dark thoughts. I felt I had no one to turn to. I was depressed and was self-medicating. The easiest way to get to sleep was to drink a bottle of wine every night. My board was hostile, though they had been all for the strategy when the stock price was going up. The stress and exhaustion were taking their toll. After six months, I was a physical and mental wreck. I had never felt this bad before. I felt like a failure at work and at home.

One night I was sitting on the lounge with my wife and was hit by massive chest pains. I couldn't breathe. I went to the emergency department at the Royal North Shore Hospital and was rushed to the cardio ward. I thought I was done for. After two days of tests, the results came back: I hadn't had a heart attack, but I did have acute pericarditis, which is an inflammation of the fibrous sac surrounding my heart. I was told it was most likely the result of being run down. Two Nurofen later and I was right for discharge. I kid you not!

For me, this was a wake-up call. It was time to make a change. That crisis forced me to think about what was really important to me: my health, my family and things other than work. It was time to put my life into perspective. I took some time off and got a personal trainer — Dan Adair, an absolute legend. He kicked my arse and got my diet in order. I lost 30 kilos, did the run leg of a corporate triathlon and am now the fittest and healthiest I have ever been. Oh, and I resigned from REFFIND.

Although it had a terrible personal impact on both me and my family, this experience changed my life for the better. It taught me an enormous amount about what it takes to be physically, mentally and emotionally fit enough to run a startup. I learned it the hard way — firsthand.

THE STAKES ARE HIGH

When we think about startup failure, the first thing that comes to mind is the financial impact — investors losing their money, which is terrible. But we sometimes forget the human impact — on founders and on the teams they lead. I've experienced this personally. I know and have spoken with many other founders who face a tremendous amount of stress and pressure. They have put their personal reputations on the line with investors and with their teams. They must deal with the fear of failure, the risk of public embarrassment, negative articles in the press, even hostile investors showing up at their homes. I've known founders who are massively depressed, even suicidal.

But it's not only founders. Many people are affected. When startups fail, people lose their jobs. They must go home and tell their partner that the startup they were working for has gone under and they need to find a new job. Startup failure has an enormous human impact. Reducing it not only decreases financial loss but ensures we will have founders and teams with innovative ideas who are willing to come back for a second try. We want to keep that talent in the startup ecosystem.

FOUNDER FATIGUE: THE ELEPHANT IN THE ROOM

Part of my motivation for writing this book is to call out the elephant in the room: I call it *founder fatigue*. It's almost taboo to talk about the human aspects of business, but they are real. I see founders struggling with this, thinking, 'Should I stay unemotional? Should I be impervious to this stress?' The reality is that most founders suffer stress in one form or another, and it's a lonely place to be if you don't have a support network around you.

To a certain degree, our business environment tries to take the human element out of the workplace. There are unspoken rules: no tears at work; you shouldn't even be angry at work. I suggest that's just impossible to achieve because businesses are full of human beings. But it's important to get out in front of it. When you put a small team in a high-pressure environment you can get a lot of conflict and toxicity. With the right mindset, on the other hand, you can have teams that work exceptionally well together.

Most first-time founders come from the corporate world, where companies usually shy away from this level of introspection. They don't have to deal with it. If you're in a company with 5000 people, there are so many cogs in the machine; there are processes and systems that buffer the organisation from the ebbs and flows of the individual's mood swings. One person's impact in a corporate environment is far less than it might be in a startup where the teams are small and each individual's contribution is much greater.

The conventional wisdom is that founders need to be like Apple's CEO, the late Steve Jobs, or the product architect of Tesla Motors, Elon Musk, or Facebook's Mark Zuckerberg. Idolised as they are, it is easy to forget they are human beings with flaws and failings like everyone else.

EXTERNAL PRESSURE

Adding to the pressure that founders place on themselves is the pressure exerted on them by their boards and by investors. There is an unfortunate recurring theme in startups: many founders are dumped by their own boards or by the investors who initially backed them. This is far from uncommon. Steve Jobs (Apple), Travis Kalanick (Uber), Andrew Mason (Groupon), Jerry Yang (Yahoo), Rod Canion (Compaq) and Jack Dorsey (Twitter) are just a few examples.

Various reasons and justifications are given, some of them fair, some not. Sometimes they are just looking for a scapegoat or a change. Whatever the reality, this historical pattern means founders are often wary of their boards and their investors, and often obsess over control. It further cements the importance of choosing your boards and your investors wisely. Regardless of the reasons, it is a mistake to lose founder DNA from a company.

BE PREPARED

Being physically, mentally and emotionally ready as a founder is critically important. Long experience has taught me that an incredible amount of stress is placed on founders. If you're not physically and mentally ready for it, it can have a horrible personal impact. Insomnia, depression, anger, lashing out at others — if you're not ready for the pressure, the process of founding and operating a startup is going to suck.

As a founder, you are normally focused on your product, your business model, your team, the competition — everything but yourself. With 270 other things on your to-do list, reviewing your own strengths and weaknesses is usually the last thing on your mind.

I suggest you need to come first. It's all about being prepared. There is a motto in the military: 'Train hard; fight easy'. If you have thought through the challenges, and prepared for them, then the actual events will be way simpler to deal with. If you're ready, you'll be calmer, more energised and less stressed, and you'll be able to keep both your physical and mental wellbeing in a good place too.

Myth: You need to work 24/7

There is no doubt that startups are about hustle. It should be an endeavour that you're passionate about and want to spend significant amounts of time on. But too many founders burn themselves out. With founder fatigue you are no use to anyone — you can't lead your team effectively, and you won't make the best decisions. The startup community is moving away from the view that founders are expected to work themselves to the bone. Hustle, yes — just don't wipe yourself out.

CAPACITY + CAPABILITY = FOUNDER FITNESS

To be a great founder you need both capacity and capability. Often founders work only on building capability — that is, learning the specific skills they need to do the job. While having these skills is essential, having the capacity to go the distance is far more important. Capacity gives you reserves. It's your fuel tank. It provides you with a solid foundation on which to build skills.

The Founder Fitness model (figure 6.1) focuses on building capacity in three key areas:

- physical
- mental
- emotional.

FIGURE 6.1: FOUNDER FITNESS MODEL

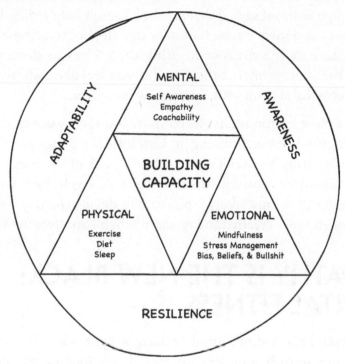

LET'S GET PHYSICAL

Given the intensity and focus required to found a startup, a lot of entrepreneurs slip into the habit of ignoring their health and wellbeing. They stop exercising, eat poorly and operate on minimal sleep. It's crucial to be in great shape as a founder; you need your body to go the distance. Having been extremely unfit for a large part of my career, I know this firsthand. You don't need to become a professional athlete or gym junkie, but getting yourself in decent shape will serve you well.

You also need to give the 'startup diet' of beer and pizza a miss. It's so easy to cut corners and eat badly, cramming down something quick and easy at lunch, then countless dinners with investors and prospects, but it all adds inches to your waistline and means you'll be lugging around more than just your new product ideas every day. It should go without saying that alcohol doesn't help either. I know from direct experience how founders use alcohol to self-medicate, whether to ease the stress or to drink themselves to sleep. It may work in the short term, but the next day you feel like crap. You can't run a successful startup with a perpetual hangover.

Last, but most important, is sleep. Many founders wear exhaustion like a badge of honour, boasting on how little sleep they get. Sleep is the wonder drug. You can't operate 24/7. Lack of sleep makes you irritable and means you will function well below your best. Get your sleep, even if it means taking a power nap during the day. I know I feel so much more creative and resilient when I am sleeping well.

EMPATHY IS THE NEW BLACK: MENTAL FITNESS

Some would say I don't mind picking a fight when it comes to challenging startup founders. In fact, I am looking to see how mentally fit they are. What best indicates mental fitness for me is *coachability*. When a founder pitches me a startup, I look for cues that indicate how coachable they are. It is a critical factor in determining whether or not I will invest.

Being coachable comes down to a number of factors. It starts with how self-aware you are. This quality often develops as you get older, but I have met many young self-aware founders who are coachable. How well do you know yourself and what makes you tick? What gets you out of bed in the morning? What are you good at and what drives you crazy? Are you self-aware enough to build a team around you who complement your strengths and offset your weaknesses? Can you keep your ego in check? Do you understand how you will deal with failure but also how to deal with success? I've seen success go to a founder's head, making them arrogant and unpleasant to work with.

In his bestselling book *Emotional Intelligence*, Dan Goleman discusses the concept of EQ, or emotional intelligence. People with high EQ have the ability to recognise their emotional responses and to manage and adapt them depending on the environment. They also have a high level of empathy, which can be defined as the ability to understand and share the feelings of others. A well-developed ability to empathise with others sets great startup founders apart. Being empathetic improves your ability to lead and motivate a team, and increases your capacity to craft a fantastic product for your customers through understanding the problem they are trying to solve.

Being coachable also manifests in how well you take criticism. One technique I often employ when being pitched to by founders is to criticise one aspect of their idea or business. The response is always enlightening. Some founders go straight on the offensive, hitting back without even listening to what I've said. Others fall silent. The answer I am looking for is 'Why do you think that?' I'm looking for a sense of curiosity and openness, as demonstrated by founders who try to understand *why* I am criticising their idea. Those founders are coachable. Being able to listen and respond to criticism will help your startup, especially if the critique is coming from someone who has experience in your field. It doesn't mean you can't be passionate. The world needs passionate founders. But if you are so passionate that you aren't willing to listen to feedback, you will leave a lot of great advice on the table.

This leads me to my pet hate when it comes to founder behavioural traits: arrogance combined with ignorance. When I come across a founder who is both inexperienced and arrogant, I run for the hills. There is no single clearer indicator that a founder will nuke a startup than this. It is a ridiculously dangerous combination. Founders who exhibit these traits are usually grounded in one or more of the startup myths. They underappreciate the skill and dedication that is required to be successful, and they have an ego that is out of control.

These founders are uncoachable and reckless, flying by the seat of their pants and destroying relationships both inside and outside of their company.

Life is way too short to work with these kinds of founders. Luckily most of them never get funding.

FEAR IS THE MIND KILLER: EMOTIONAL FITNESS

If there's one word that encapsulates the startup founder experience, it's fear. Fear of failure. Fear of disappointing your team and your investors. When you raise capital, many of your investors are investing in *you*, especially in the early stages of the business. They could be friends and family or well-regarded angel investors. You're putting yourself and your personal brand on the line. And others are trusting that you will be successful and won't let them down. I know what it's like to have people you know and care about lose money. It sucks.

It's exciting to be funded, but once you are it can be incredibly scary. You think the only way to quell that fear is to work around the clock like a complete lunatic. You feel a terrible burden and sense of responsibility. Just dealing with the fear can be a hurdle for some. You need to stay focused, confident that if you build a business on a solid idea and with a solid business model, you have a good chance of success.

Knowing that you're going to experience this fear is the first step. Don't worry. You're not alone. Everyone has a fear of failure, of disappointing people, of letting your team down. It's important to acknowledge the fear, but not to let it overwhelm you.

Sometimes the fear drives self-doubt. Are you good enough to do this? Mike Cannon-Brookes, co-founder of Atlassian (a fully certified Unicorn), has spoken about *imposter syndrome*. At a recent TEDx talk he put it like this:

> Have you ever felt out of your depth, like a fraud, and just kind of guessed-slash-bullshitted your way through the situation, petrified that at any time someone was going to call you on it? It's not a fear of failure. It's not a fear of being unable to do it. It's more a sensation of getting away with something, a fear of being discovered, that at any time someone is going to figure it out.

Successful or not, it's natural for startup founders sometimes to have a sense of self-doubt or anxiety. Dealing with it requires a combination of preparation and mental attitude. This book and other resources will help you build competence. Knowing the blueprint to building a successful startup will go a long way to reducing the anxiety you feel when you don't know what to do and are working in the dark. Develop a healthy mental attitude and resilience. That attitude is partly self-confidence, but self-awareness is even more important than confidence. Having the right mindset helps.

A FITNESS TEST

To help you prepare for what lies ahead, it's time for some hard questions. Here are 10 questions you should ask yourself:

1. How physically fit am I? Can I afford to lose some weight? When was the last time I went to a gym or did some exercise?

2. How good is my diet? Am I indulging in too many boozy work lunches? Do I eat comfort food when I am stressed?

3. What does my alcohol intake look like? Am I drinking too much to deal with the pressure?

4. Am I getting enough sleep? When was the last time I got a good night's sleep? Do I suffer from insomnia? Do I need to take pills to help me sleep?

5. How calm am I? Do I meditate? Am I willing to give it a try?

6. Do I have a hobby or outlet outside of work? Am I able to switch off or am I in a constant state of anxiety, waiting for the next email?

7. How are my relationships? Am I spending enough time with my partner and family and giving them the attention they deserve?

8. How have I historically dealt with stress and pressure? Can I recognise when I am stressed, and do I have strategies to deal with it?

9. How do I handle criticism? Am I open to it, or do I shut down and get defensive?

10. Have I ever suffered a major setback? How did I react to it? How did it affect me emotionally and physically? What did I learn from it?

Start with some introspection; it is good practice. How do you deal with a crisis? How do you deal with criticism? What leadership role are you going to play in a team? This is about developing your EQ and getting to know yourself better, and building self-awareness.

Then have some conversations with your family — your partner, your wife, your girlfriend, your husband. You might say, 'Hey, potentially this could be a very stressful time. I'm going to need your support.' Having these honest exchanges before things go too far can go a long way to protecting and even strengthening those relationships.

OVER TO YOU:
3 STEPS TO BECOMING
A FITTER FOUNDER

As a founder, you need to look out for your fitness, both physical and mental. Your team and your investors are counting on you to go the distance, so spend time on yourself in order that you can help others. Here are three things you can do that will help you to build resilience, awareness and adaptability.

STEP 1: GET PHYSICALLY FIT

It's time to get a sweat on. You need a base level of physical fitness to run a startup. Eat a healthy diet, take regular exercise and get plenty of good-quality sleep at night. It's hard to deal with high levels of stress if you're not physically well. An honest assessment of your physical health is the place to start.

You don't have to become a triathlete, but starting a basic fitness program is going to help you tremendously. Join a gym — hire a personal trainer if you need that extra push — or just start walking every morning. Good eating habits are even more important. I've eaten countless of crap work lunches, washed down with bottles of red wine, that not only piled on the weight but slowed me down mentally.

You need to be physically fit enough to deal with the day-to-day demands you place on your body.

STEP 2: GET MENTALLY FIT

Stress test your mental and emotional fitness. How do you respond to criticism? How do you deal with stress? How have you dealt with stressful events in the past? Have you started a business before? What was the most stressful event in your life? Do you feel that you understand how difficult and stressful this is going to be? How have you dealt with past failure in your life?

Pause, reflect and clear yourself some mental space. The best way to do this is through meditation. If you haven't tried it before, I recommend it. You don't need to become a monk. Even 10 minutes of meditation a day can have a huge impact. There are great apps out there — my favourites are Headspace and Smiling Mind — apps that you can download onto your smartphone or tablet to make learning to meditate fun and easy.

Consider getting a life coach. Lots of people find it useful to talk things through regularly with a neutral person. It can be a great emotional and mental outlet. Choose someone who allows you to unload some of your issues and talk through decisions, fears and other worries, someone who won't be judgemental and who can provide an outside view.

STEP 3: SWITCH OFF

One important element in your overall wellness will be your ability to switch off. By their nature, most startup founders are obsessive compulsive and think about their business 24 hours a day and seven days a week. Most are adrenaline junkies who feed off the energy and fast tempo. But this constant state of mental alertness takes its toll. I understand this all too well, as I find it hugely difficult to switch off.

Top athletes know that to achieve peak performance they need to have rest days and an off-season that gives them time to recover and regenerate. It's no different in business. Running at

100 per cent for extended periods is not okay. As impossible as it may seem to you, you need to learn to switch off — at both a micro and a macro level.

What this means will differ for each person. Some people prefer to work in the evenings; some find their mornings more productive. Whatever your preferred working style, it's important to take some time away from work every single week to rest and recover. Devote this time to people and activities that aren't work related. Catch up with friends and family, pursue a hobby or sport — anything that allows you to switch off.

At a macro level, it's important to schedule regular annual holidays so you can reset. It usually takes me three or four days off work to even get to a place where I can enjoy a holiday. Make sure you take enough time off to be fully rested. Don't feel guilty about taking time off. Develop the mindset of a performance athlete, and when you return to work, you will be more refreshed and better positioned for the next big challenge.

RECAP

The more you know about yourself and how you react under pressure, the greater your chances of business success. How are you going to respond when things go bad? Learn more about yourself, so you can better interact with others and respond positively to events when things don't work out well in your startup. Self-awareness and preparation are the keys to successful relationships.

Understand that it's all about 'train hard, fight easy'. The more physically, mentally and emotionally fit you are going into a startup, then the better you will weather the inevitable storms. This preparation will give you the strength and confidence you need. You may even relish stressful events, rather than fearing them, because you will have the tools you need both to anticipate the issues and to deal with them effectively when they occur.

WHAT'S NEXT

In the next chapter, we're going to explore a practical process that will help you build your startup from the bottom up. It's a structure that will help you build a world-class business. And, strange as it may seem, we'll discover that there is a lot we can learn from Hollywood.

CHAPTER 7
HOLLYWOOD GOT IT RIGHT

Now you are aware of the myths surrounding startups, you'll want to know where to focus your efforts to succeed. Here we are going to compare the way the companies in America's famous film-making hub, Hollywood, and those in the hotbed of startup culture, Silicon Valley, go about their business. They have more in common than you might think. Essentially, both Hollywood executives and tech founders bring together a team of creative people to produce a commercial product. A notable difference is in the failure rates, with the movie industry enjoying much lower rates than Silicon Valley startups. I'm interested in why this is so.

The best way for me to explain it to you is through an example. Roll up *Jurassic Park*! It's a story that I use often when speaking to founders. For me, the analogy is this: most people have seen this film. Technically it's a 'Unicorn', having grossed more than a billion dollars at the box office.

As you may know, the film was based on a novel by Michael Crichton. Most people who have seen the movie haven't read the book, but what is interesting to understand is the journey the book took on its way to becoming a blockbuster movie. There are parallels every step of the way between the Hollywood way and the startup process. Let's begin by thinking about the book itself and comparing it to your startup idea.

Crichton's idea was simple: bring dinosaurs back to life. The novel sold over 12 million copies. But a best-selling book based on a brilliant idea does not in itself make a billion-dollar movie.

Between the book's being optioned for a film treatment and the movie release, a host of people were involved in the project. Filming alone required a huge crew, cast, sets, sound, music, post-production, special effects and much more. You only need to look at the credits of the movie to understand how many people are involved. The credits don't just say 'by Michael Crichton'!

Making a movie is a technical and creative endeavour that requires the collaboration of many specialists. Film financing depends on venture capital.

IT AIN'T SHOW FRIENDS, IT'S SHOW BUSINESS

And business is something Hollywood is very good at. They have been perfecting their model for almost 100 years, and there's no doubt it works. It is estimated that between 50 and 64 per cent of Hollywood movies make a profit, a far cry from the 8 per cent for technology startups. I put the difference down to what I call the Hollywood Method™. I believe it's worth examining the structure and method used in Hollywood to build a creative, commercially viable product.

I meet many founders who come to the startup game with no structure to their plans. All they know is they need to build a technological 'solution'; they don't yet know how to produce that product, let alone find a profitable market for it. The Hollywood Method provides us with a map and a proven structure when creating a product that people want. It offers us a methodical, structured approach to analysing what people want, how to develop that product, then how to market and distribute it in a way that minimises both cost and risk.

It's an approach that is sure to broaden your perspective as a startup founder. You will come to understand, 'There's a lot of work I need to do before I start developing my product.' It means you will take fewer risks, do a lot less rework and, most importantly, suffer a lot less frustration. Using your capital more wisely and cost-effectively, you'll maximise your chances of success, because every dollar you spend will take you a step closer to the great company and product you want to create.

If you are not familiar with the way Hollywood makes movies, the entire process is encompassed in four broad phases — development, pre-production, production and post-production (figure 7.1). Each of these phases is completed sequentially, the time required for each phase varying according to the particular movie.

FIGURE 7.1: THE FOUR PHASES OF HOLLYWOOD MOVIE MAKING

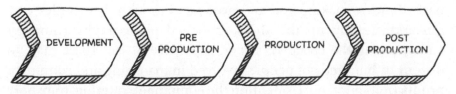

DEVELOPMENT

The first phase is development. The predominant activities here are story development, working on script ideas, writing and rewriting the screenplay, and starting to think about funding. This phase is sometimes referred to as 'development hell', as it is marked by much painful trial and error, with initial concepts and scripts critiqued and frequently rejected or reworked. This, by the way, is a good thing. It is where Hollywood producers look at the feasibility of a particular project, taking into account the current appetite for particular genres, the quality of the script and what talent is available. A movie that meets the studio's requirements will get the green light and move into pre-production.

PRE-PRODUCTION

Pre-production is the critical planning and preparation phase of a movie project. Actors are cast, locations scouted, storyboards and shot lists created. By turning the script into storyboards, the team get to visualise the movie and begin to make decisions on camera angles and framing and countless other elements. In recent years, hand-drawn storyboards have been supplemented by digital pre-visualisation techniques, such as low-fidelity animation, to help the team to visualise the final product — all without shooting a single frame of footage.

PRODUCTION

Lights, camera, action! The production phase is most likely the part of movie making you are most familiar with. It includes cast rehearsal, setting up the shots, principal photography (filming) and checking the takes. This is an expensive phase. There may be dozens or hundreds of people involved in managing and running a production shoot, not to mention the equipment, catering, transport and accommodation. For this reason, film-makers know to keep this phase as short and tight as possible. It might be the iconic aspect of movie production, but they burn money during this phase, so Hollywood knows to get it done as quickly and efficiently as possible.

POST-PRODUCTION

That's a wrap! After filming comes the post-production phase. This includes editing the various takes into a final cohesive form, adding any digital effects, incorporating the sound effects and the musical soundtrack. This is about assembly and polish. Once a final cut of the movie is completed test screenings will sometimes be arranged, which allow the studio to gauge audience reception. If it isn't great, then adjustments may be made, with scenes re-edited or reshot (introducing a different ending, for example), but this isn't a great outcome. If the movie isn't right by this stage, then it is likely to have a more fundamental problem.

SHOW ME THE MONEY!

Hollywood executives are exceptionally good at being tight with their budgets. Yes, they spend a lot of money producing movies, but they spend it when they need to, at the right time. The most common mistake I see founders make is choosing the wrong time to spend. They want to produce an app, so they start off by sourcing some money from friends, family or fans (in what is called an F3 capital round), or they pay for this part of the process themselves (called bootstrapping). Then they usually hire a freelance developer and start to build the app. They waste a lot of money this way. I've seen founders burn through up to a million dollars and go broke building their app. Ouch.

Not an ideal approach. So let's see what Hollywood does. First, they don't go, 'Jurassic Park! That's a smashing idea! Let's make and film some dinosaurs. Get the cameras out, let's go.' Hollywood knows that the most expensive part of making a movie happens when the cameras come out. Look at all the people who are needed to run a set. There are the actors, directors, runners, gaffers, catering, the sound, costume and makeup people — the list goes on and on. Instead, what Hollywood does is spend a long time in the planning and preparation phases.

You can apply the same process to your startup. Take your idea and start building your business model (which is your screenplay). Ask yourself, 'What am I trying to achieve here? How is it going to work in practice? What's the story of my product?' You can start to build some wireframes and prototypes.

BE TOM CRUISE, NOT CLINT EASTWOOD

I'm sure you are familiar with the actors Tom Cruise and Clint Eastwood. I would suggest that most founders try to be Clint Eastwood, when they really should be Tom Cruise. Bear with me.

Clint Eastwood is an amazing actor and director, and also an accomplished producer and writer. He is a Unicorn in his own right, and in Hollywood an exception to the rule. Tom Cruise is best known for his specialisation — and has starred in a huge number of profitable movies, mostly thrillers, from *Top Gun* to *Mission Impossible*. He is bankable, a specialist.

Hollywood is an industry of specialists. It's where people come together to bring their combined expertise to a specific endeavour. If you are the director of photography, you're not going to direct films, or write them. Michael Crichton wrote another dozen blockbuster books. He focused his time and energy. Crichton wrote for the TV show *ER*, wrote and directed the film *Westworld*, and produced scripts for the sequels to *Jurassic Park*. He wrote many high-profile, successful novels and screenplays because he applied himself to what he was good at.

Hollywood studios will choose different directors (leaders) to suit particular movies. Each film requires an extraordinary director, just as each startup requires particular kinds of founders and leaders. If you want to make a science fiction movie, you get J. J. Abrams or Steven Spielberg to direct. If you want to make a drama, you might ask Clint Eastwood. Author Michael Crichton didn't direct *Jurassic Park*; he didn't act in it or film it either. Directors and producers are a good match for certain types of movies, and the same goes for startups. Just because you came up with the idea and business model, it doesn't mean you are the best person to lead the company or oversee every aspect of your startup. Why do you think you're best equipped to be the director or operate the sound mixing desk or be the director of photography?

Once you have launched your startup and seen it through its early stages, it's okay to hand over the reins to someone else and focus on your next project. It is much better for you to be producing two, three, four great startups and doing what you're good at than thinking you have to sit here and do all these things you don't enjoy. It's a team endeavour, and it's all about getting specialists together for the different aspects of the project.

ROLL THE CREDITS

Michael Crichton was not solely responsible for the billion-dollar blockbuster movie produced from the film rights. Crichton was one component of it. Even director Steven Spielberg cannot claim exclusive responsibility for its incredible success. Count the number of people listed in the credits of *Jurassic Park* and you will reach a total in the high hundreds. The sound design of *Tyrannosaurus rex*'s roar reportedly involved a composite of tiger, alligator and baby elephant sounds. The deadly *Dilophosaurus*'s roar combined howler monkey growls, hawk screeches, rattlesnake hisses and swan calls. The noises of seven quite different animals were used to create just one tiny aspect of the soundscape. You understand me, right?

I have stressed the importance of your team. By now you know I have no time for the 'Super Founder' myth. The image of the lone, all-knowing founder, very popular in the press, is neither authentic nor helpful. Hollywood has a great method for managing talent that is worth emulating in the startup game. Let me explain.

They scale their teams over time according to where they are in the process. I have said that creating a movie is a collaborative process. Dynamically assembling a team, and spinning the team up and down as needed, is where Hollywood excels. In its earliest stages only a handful of people are engaged. That changes in the pre-production phase, the numbers skyrocket during production, then fall away in post-production, before dropping to zero in distribution — Hollywood outsources this part.

The other interesting thing about Hollywood is that people work in the same teams time and time again. The director moves from one movie to the next, from *Jurassic Park* to *Schindler's List*. So he thinks, 'Well, I worked with that sound guy on *Jurassic Park* and he was awesome, so I want him to come and work with me on this production. I worked with those writers on *Indiana Jones*. Sarah is a great writer; I want her to come and work with me on *Saving Private Ryan*.'

HOLLYWOOD VS SILICON VALLEY

As I have said numerous times, a startup is in constant search of a profitable, scalable business model. Once it finds one, it ceases to be a startup. It is highly unlikely that a startup founder's idea and business model will be perfect straight out of the box. A lot of founders think they are visionaries — most of them are hallucinating. Ultimately, until you prove your assumptions true or false in the market, you are only guessing on who your customers will be, and whether they will actually pay for your business model. Hollywood's method, and the approach I will teach you in next chapter, allows you to test your assumptions as quickly and economically as possible. Remember, most startups are default dead, so you need to solve your cash burn problem as quickly and efficiently as possible.

Proving your assumptions is about *fit*. There are three main kinds of fit.

The first is *problem/solution fit*. This is really about validating whether or not you have a good idea. Many first-time founders operate in a vacuum. Once you have identified the problem you are trying to solve, get out there and find some prospective customers. You need prospective customers who say they 'must have' a solution to the problem you are trying to solve. And not just a couple of them — the more the better, but preferably at least 10 to 20. Then you need them to say they 'must have' *your* solution to that problem. If you have this, then you have problem/solution fit. But be careful. This is only the first step, and it is only a 'paper fit'. It's one thing for customers to agree on paper to wanting your product, but quite another for them to put their hands in their pockets when you show up with a real product.

The second kind of fit is known as *product/market fit*. This term was originally coined by noted entrepreneur and VC Andy Rachleff, essentially to describe the situation when a substantial number of customers see enough real value in your product and its features that they are prepared to pay for it. It is important to nail product/market fit before thinking about scale. As Rachleff puts it, 'If the dogs don't want to eat the dog food, then what good is attracting a lot of dogs?'

It is often said that it is difficult to determine exactly when you have product/market fit, and many attempts have been made to arrive at an exact measure. I would suggest, however, that if you are honest with yourself you will know when you have it. When your product satisfies a burning customer need, they will beat a path to your door. Sales cycles are usually a great indication. If you are seeing long sales cycles and a lot of customer resistance, then you probably don't have product/market fit. If the customers are saying, 'Take my money — please', then happy days! Marc Andreessen has said, 'In a great market — a market with lots of real potential customers — the market pulls product out of the startup.' You can feel product/market fit.

The last kind of fit is *business model fit*, which is really about your growth hypothesis. Customer demand alone does not make a successful startup. Once you have achieved product/market fit, is your business model profitable? And does it scale? This is business model fit. Once you have product/market fit you can focus on business model fit. How do you acquire customers profitably? How can you do this at scale and not go broke?

In short, you are not smarter than your customers. The market always wins and the market is always right. The Hollywood Method allows you to find that market, and gain fit quickly and cost-effectively.

CASE STUDY: BEAUTY IS IN THE EYE OF THE BEHOLDER

I once worked with a startup that created a product in the health and beauty sector. They developed an application that could be described as Uber for beauty therapists. Their initial value proposition was based on the assumption that clients would like to connect with various beauty therapists (think hair, nails, tan etc.) on an on-demand basis. The startup was making some progress, but in my view the initial value proposition didn't seem to resonate fully with customers.

There were some questions that still needed to be answered. For example, do people really want a different therapist every single time? Is this indeed an activity that people want 'on-demand' or is it something they would prefer to schedule? The founders went back and did more research and testing with prospective customers 'outside the building'. As a result, they focused down on hotel guests (who don't mind a new therapist) and developed more scheduling functionality. The lesson here is that as a startup you should be looking to test and prove your assumptions continually.

DESIGN THINKING VS THE HOLLYWOOD METHOD

When researching the best way to solve customer problems you will come across the terms 'human-centred design' and 'design thinking'. I am a huge advocate of design thinking. It's a great methodology that I have studied and applied extensively. It is not strictly applicable to startups, however.

Design thinking is better suited to corporations. It is a great hands-on research tool, but it starts with the customer as a known data point. Established companies, who have a very good understanding of who their customers are, can use design thinking methods to better determine the needs of those customers when looking to create new and innovative products. These companies already have a business model — they are looking to enhance and expand that model.

By contrast, startups are in search of a business model, and more importantly a product/market fit. Starting out with a value proposition and/or technology in mind, they need to quickly find customers and a market for that value proposition, to test and adapt it, and to get traction and revenue quickly.

Startups, being default dead, have a finite amount of money and time. So the methods and techniques they use need to deliver results fast and be very focused on solving the one problem every startup founder faces — how do I find a viable business model before I run out of cash? Corporates, on the other hand, usually (though not always) have more time, and they almost certainly have more money. They can afford to take their time with design thinking processes in order to derive insights into their existing customers.

That said, design thinking focuses on customer empathy, which is a core building block when creating a desirable value proposition. You can still learn great techniques and adopt the tools of design thinking — just don't get distracted from your main objective.

IT'S ABOUT MARKET FIT, NOT PRODUCT

Just as Hollywood is synonymous with movies, tech startups are synonymous with their technology — so much so that it can blind founders to everything else. The product is tangible, visible; it's something everyone gravitates towards and works on. The technology is a siren song for founders, who are magnetically attracted to their products. Of course, products are essential, but that siren song means that founders overlook other important areas such as market and customer research, product planning, storyboarding, prototyping and testing. It's often easier to go and work on your product than it is to work on anything else.

The lack of awareness around this parallel with Hollywood is the main reason I wrote this book. The first two phases of product development are not understood in a mature and developed way by many founders. To understand this well means learning how to do market research — to ask questions to identify market needs, to ask customers why they do certain things. Understanding consumer behaviour is still an emerging aspect of the industry right now.

For this reason, when most startups first learn about software development life cycles, they focus on how to make a product efficiently. And they learn this before they have research results confirming that their business model is sound. It is tempting to focus on product, but there is a widespread lack of knowledge around customer development. Which is why I am providing founders with a structured approach for the process. What I'm proposing is a comprehensive map, and a descriptive, prescriptive approach to structuring your thinking and actions, and to navigating the life cycle of your startup.

Myth: The best technical product wins

Products that were technically amazing but tanked anyway litter the startup world. You could think about these startups as equivalent to Hollywood's epic flop *Waterworld*. Great products alone don't win customers and markets. Why do some technically great products fail while less impressive products succeed? In my experience, startup teams that devote significant time to understanding the problem they are solving, conduct well-executed customer research, and produce a product that meets the minimum customer requirements, outperform startups that only obsess over product features. The way to build a successful product is to collect feedback and secure customer validation as quickly as possible. Iterating on a minimum viable product (MVP) is the only way to include the 'customer's voice' in your product and to develop a product that customers want to pay for — which, frankly, is the name of the game.

Steve Jobs famously said, 'Real artists ship!' Once you are confident that your product solves a real problem, and you have validated your solution with the target customer base, ship it. I've seen a lot of startups that are paralysed by the pursuit of perfection. Your product will never be perfect. It will be in a constant state of adjustment and improvement — ideally, based on customer feedback. The sooner you can get it into the hands of your customers, the sooner you will start getting that valuable feedback. In this sense, perfection is the enemy of success.

RECAP

Hollywood has been doing this for decades and can offer the perfect methodology for a startup. As founders, we all tend to think we have no roadmap to follow, but we can draw on the experience of Hollywood movie making to improve our chances of startup success. Once you get it, you'll understand that you don't have to reinvent the wheel. You just need to follow the process. You may give birth to a billion-dollar Unicorn or to a failure, but it should be an inexpensive failure, not one that will break you.

Why Hollywood? Essentially, Hollywood incubates startups. Every movie is a startup that brings together a large team of creative people to produce a commercial product based on an idea. Hollywood has been far more successful at this than Silicon Valley. Startup founders can learn much from this success. With limited capital, you need to spend it wisely. As a founder you can reduce your risk by good planning and preparation before production. Following the Hollywood Method, you will spend more time planning and ensuring that what you build is what your market wants. That will make for happy customers and increase your chances of success.

WHAT'S NEXT

In the next chapter, we're going to take a deep dive into the Hollywood Method and look at how it can be applied to startups. We will explore the four phases of the method and the essential skills you will need to apply it successfully as a founder. We'll review the process, the tools and the pitfalls, and see how, by applying the method, you will be better equipped for startup success.

CHAPTER 8

THE HOLLYWOOD METHOD™

G iven the fast-growing app economy and the sexiness associated with the building phase, it's not surprising that most founders rush to develop their technology. They think the startup *is* the technology. I have a different view. I think of startups rather as business models and the technology is to a certain degree irrelevant.

Let me back this up. Several years ago I worked with a first-time startup founder. He was an expert in his particular field but had never before built a technology product or a startup. Nevertheless, he raised about $1 million in funding — then spent all that money on building his product. He had used an outsourced developer who had essentially responded to every change he made — not an uncommon scenario. At the end of that process the product was terrible, because it didn't meet the needs of the customer.

After building a product that no one wanted, he had blown all his seed money and he came to me looking for more. I had to confront him with why he was in this situation: 'Your product is terrible; it doesn't meet the market need. You won't get any more funding.'

Basically, his startup went out of business the very next day, which of course had a huge personal impact on him.

His mistake was that he'd spent all his time and money on building an app without any blueprint, without a value proposition, without a business model, and certainly without a prototype. He'd spent hundreds of thousands of dollars on outsourced developers, who were just coding away at his instruction, to build a product with no plan, no market and no customer. It was an exceptionally costly mistake — indeed a terminal one for his startup — all because he made the mistake of rushing to build.

Myth: You don't need a plan

Although they are usually disruptive, startups still need a plan. I often see startups that have no discipline or rigour around how they're going about finding a scalable, repeatable, profitable business model. Completely misconstruing the Lean Startup movement, they use the idea of 'iteration' as a crutch. Their approach is often along the lines of, 'If we just iterate on the product, everything's going to be okay'. Well, usually it's not okay. All startups need at least a test plan outlining how they are going to test their value proposition and business model hypotheses (which are no more than best guesses at this stage) and how they are going to respond to the outcome of those tests. Startups can't defy gravity. They still need a plan, even if not the kind of plan you see in a large corporation.

THERE IS NO FOUNDER MANUAL

There is no manual for being a startup founder. To a certain degree you need simply to make the best decisions possible at any given point. The professionalism and expertise expected of founders has increased in recent years. The bar has been raised. Investors demand it, and so do employees. They don't expect a founder just to wander around in the wilderness. They expect a structured approach that means you can communicate the purpose behind every decision you make. If you change a product feature, for example, all your stakeholders — investors and staff — will want to know why. They will also want a clear understanding of your vision and plans for the future are. You are a leader — that is what leaders do.

Communicating to investors and to your team the path you are on will reduce their level of anxiety. They will feel more confidence in you as a founder if they know you're following a structured and methodical approach rather than just throwing darts at a board and hoping everything works out. 'Hope', as a wise man once said, 'is not a strategy.' (It was the former New York City mayor Rudy Giuliani, if you are interested.)

EMPATHY IS MORE IMPORTANT THAN TECHNOLOGY (FOR NOW)

The early stages of a tech company are not technology dependent. Planning involves getting out and interviewing your customer and developing a deep understanding of them. Then it's a matter of building a value proposition and a business model. Those steps do not depend on technology. There are no answers in the building. You need to get out and observe your prospective customers in their natural environment.

It's down to a lot of legwork, the tried-and-true path. One skill that will help you a great deal is empathy, your capacity to understand and share the feelings of others. Developing strong empathy for your prospective customers is the foundation of the Hollywood Method. Think of it as understanding your audience. Who are they? Where do they live? Where do they work? What are their hopes and fears? What drives them? Being able to 'walk a mile in their shoes' means you will have them at the centre of your business model, where they will influence and even determine the design of your product.

Understanding your customers means more than just surveying them. It means getting to the heart of the reasons why they do certain things. What tasks are they trying to perform? What do they see as gains? What pain are they trying to avoid? As customers, we don't always admit to what drives us. Founders who are empathetic can more easily elicit those motivations from customers.

THE HOLLYWOOD METHOD™

I designed the Hollywood Method to help startup founders develop their idea into a profitable business. Inspired by the tested and hugely successful Hollywood movie-making system, it follows a similar four-stage approach (figure 8.1). It also draws on the growing body of knowledge around lean customer development. My aim is to present a strategy that is accessible, easy to understand and easy to follow.

FIGURE 8.1: THE HOLLYWOOD METHOD™

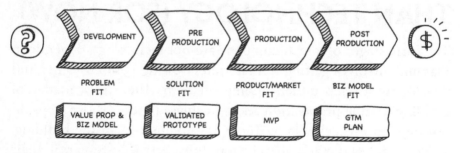

1. DEVELOPMENT

So you have an idea for a startup. Maybe it came to you as a spark of martini-induced brilliance, or perhaps you have been grinding away at it for years and have only now decided to take the plunge. Congratulations, you have taken the first step to becoming a startup founder. That was the easy part, though. Remember, everyone's got one!

Development, the first phase in building a startup using the Hollywood Method, focuses on transforming your idea into a desirable value proposition, then embedding that value proposition within a feasible business model.

It's time to get out of the building and start exploring those guesses. Formally, this is called *problem validation*. On completion of this phase you will have:

- an identified customer segment
- a value proposition for that customer segment
- a working business model
- enough real customer data to support your choices.

In this phase we are assessing problem/solution fit. Remember, this is about 'paper fit' and is only the first step. We will go on to test for product/market fit in later stages.

DEVELOP YOUR VALUE PROPOSITION

In Hollywood a lot of time is spent deciding whether to make a movie at all. Is now the right time to put out a sci-fi style western about robots working in a theme park? In the startup world this is about the value proposition. The idea needs to be turned into a value proposition, which must be embedded in a business model.

In development you need to spend a lot of time understanding who your customer is. The best way to achieve this is through ethnographic interviewing. Go and observe your customers, specifically when trying to perform the task your idea is built around. Ask them questions. Video them. Survey them online. You are trying to build up customer profile:

- What tasks are they trying to carry out?
- What gains or outcomes do they hope for?
- What pain are they trying to avoid?

Next you need to map your value proposition, linking it to those three points. How does your product or service help them carry out those tasks? What gains does it create for the customer? What pain does it relieve?

A great tool here is Osterwalder and Pigneur's Value Proposition Canvas, introduced in their book *Value Proposition Design* (discussed in chapter 4). This tool helps you to build a customer profile and a value map, and to assess how well your solution fits on paper with the customer needs.

Another tool I like using in this phase, first developed by Strategyzer, is *value proposition ad-lib statements*, which are a way of structuring value proposition alternatives through a structured sentence and can often help you collect your thoughts. The ad-lib structure looks like this:

Our [**product**]

helps [**customer segment**]

who want to [**jobs to be done**]

by reducing [**customer pain**]

and increasing [**customer gain**],

unlike [**competing value proposition**].

An example of this might be:

Our ride-sharing service helps the mass market, who want to travel from A to B, by reducing the pain of owning a car and dealing with terrible taxi drivers, and increasing convenience and quality of service, unlike using regular taxi cabs.

By articulating your value proposition using both the Value Proposition Canvas and ad-lib statements, you will able to explore different variations and hone in on what is most important for the customer.

DEVELOP YOUR BUSINESS MODEL

A value proposition is only as good as the business model it is embedded in.

Think of a value proposition as delivering value for the customer and a business model as delivering value for your business. Both are critical.

Designing a business model can be challenging, especially if you have never had to create one before. Luckily, a fast and simple way of creating business models has been developed. This is Alex Osterwalder's Business Model Canvas, discussed in chapter 4. You can read more about it in his book *Business Model Generation.*

In essence, your business model defines what your business does (what products/services you will sell to what customers) and how you will make money (your costs and what resources and revenue streams you will require). It's important to determine your business model early. Startups without a business model tend to flame out pretty quickly.

TEST/ITERATE

You may find you need to experiment and test different value propositions and business models until you find one that fits what you are trying to achieve — to deliver a product to customers that they want and value using a business model that makes money.

This is the time to go out and speak to prospective customers (speaking to your brother-in-law doesn't count). Test your thinking on them. Find out how big and how important they think the problem you are trying to solve is, and how they are currently solving it. Is it a huge pain point or just a minor inconvenience? The more customers you speak to the better. Get good at reading body language and formalise your testing process. Build up a group of target customers you can speak to frequently who are willing to provide you with feedback. They will also form the bulk of your pilot customers once you have a product to give them.

In Hollywood, development is where ideas are evaluated and kicked around before being approved ('green-lighted') for production. In the startup community founders are commonly wedded to their original idea, convinced their first startup needs to be the next Facebook. This is a mistake. Not that I don't value passionate, focused entrepreneurs, but the reality is you have choices. Most entrepreneurs have more than one idea kicking around in their head. How do you choose between them? What is the best idea to be working on right now? How do you prioritise? It's okay to be working on a number of projects. Michael Crichton wrote many books. Timing is important. This is what the development phase is about — evaluating and weighing up what project you are going to work on next, ensuring it has the greatest chance of success by tailoring the product to meet your current audience (customer).

The market is the market is the market — you can't fight it. You are not smarter than your customers. In order to win, you need to develop something that the market has a burning hunger for.

PITCHING

Once you have your value proposition and business model, it's time to start thinking about pitching. Even if you don't need funding, this can be a great exercise for clarifying your thinking. Being able to clearly and effectively communicate your value proposition can help shape your business. Put together a slide deck (no more than 10 slides) that outlines:

- ▸ the market you are addressing
- ▸ the customer you are focusing on
- ▸ the problem that customer has (and why it is important to them)

- ▸ your solution to that problem (and what makes you different)
- ▸ how you validated your problem/solution fit (what test you performed).

Potential investors and others you pitch to will all have an opinion. Don't be discouraged. Listen to this feedback. Ask lots of why questions and, if relevant, incorporate this feedback into your offering to make it stronger. Pitching is a very valuable exercise — and in this phase you are not pitching to raise capital; you are using the pitching process to consolidate your thinking and test it on a broader audience.

2. PRE-PRODUCTION

Having completed the development phase, you now have a value proposition and a business model for your startup. The next part is my personal favourite.

Pre-production is probably the most important phase of both movie and startup production. In the startup world it is given too little attention. The temptation of most entrepreneurs is to move as quickly as possible into building the product, where progress can be seen and felt. But without adequate pre-production most startups will fail.

In the pre-production phase you test your solution on customers and iterate and modify that solution until you nail it, all without the significant expense of software development.

During this phase you will validate your solution through a prototype, a basic mock-up of your product that you can test with customers.

Pre-production consists of four main activities:

1. Create a user persona and map their journey.
2. Create your wireframes.
3. Build a prototype.
4. Test your prototype.

PERSONA CREATION AND USER JOURNEY MAPPING

In user experience and technical circles you will often hear the term *persona*. A persona is a profile that represents a group of users or customers. Personas are used by designers to help create empathy during the design process. Rather than being a stereotype, a persona is an archetype based on research you have completed and data you have collected on your customers. A persona can assist you in putting yourself in your customer's shoes and deriving insights from their perspective. It helps make your customer real. You may have more than one persona depending on how many customer segments you are addressing or how granular you want to be.

A persona is not a demographic representation of your customer, though it may include demographic data — age, sex and so on. A dependence on demographics usually leads to stereotypes, whereas a persona should genuinely represent your customers.

Go ahead and create a persona for one of your customer segments.

The next step is to create a user journey map. A user journey map documents the relationship your user has with your product. The first thing you need to do is imagine what activities your customer (user) is going to perform with your product. This could be listing an online auction, ordering food online, posting a photo or any number of other activities. The activities a user needs to perform will depend largely on the product you are developing. Think of a user journey map as a storyboard that imagines and documents how your user will interact with your product and perform various actions. You use this map to help you with the next activity in pre-production — wireframing.

CREATE YOUR WIREFRAMES

A wireframe is a sketch that represents a screen of your product or application. Wireframing allows you to illustrate quickly and simply what various aspects of your product will look like and to explore different user interactions. You could draw them using pencil and paper or use more sophisticated and dedicated wireframing tools — the tool doesn't matter.

You don't need to wireframe every single screen of your application at first. Start with the main activities you identified in the user journey. Consider how the user will engage with your product. How will they enter data? How will they receive data?

There are a number of great wireframing tools on the market. I personally prefer Balsamiq Mockups (www.balsamiq.com) and Keynotopia (www.keynotopia.com), and there is also the industry standard, Sketch (www.sketchapp.com). All of these tools are easy to learn and allow you to create quick wireframes that are easily turned into prototypes for testing with customers.

Don't get caught up in trying to make your wireframes look 'finished'. The point of this exercise is not to create a polished-looking product; in fact, highly designed wireframes tend to be distracting, causing users to focus more on the design and less on the flow and interaction. That is why Balsamiq make their wireframes look hand drawn: it signifies that this is a rough-and-ready mock-up of the interface and is being used to test interaction and layout, not to represent the final design.

I usually start by building my wireframes in Balsamiq, then gradually improve the design fidelity over time.

BUILD A PROTOTYPE

Think of a prototype as a dummy version of your product that you can test with customers. Building a fully functioning product is expensive and takes time. The purpose of a prototype is to test your concepts cheaply and quickly.

There have been huge advances in prototyping tools in recent years. If you are in the hardware game, now 3D printers have become affordable you can quickly create models of your physical product.

If you are in the software game, it's even easier. There is a plethora of tools you can use to turn your wireframes into what looks like a fully functioning application.

My personal favourite is InVision (www.invisionapp.com), which is an affordable tool that allows you to connect your wireframe screens together to create a 'fake app' that you then download to your phone or simulate in a web browser. If done properly, these prototypes can often be indistinguishable from the real thing, making them a hugely valuable tool for customer testing.

My advice is to increase the fidelity of your prototype gradually. By fidelity, I mean how finished it looks. A low-fidelity prototype may be a series of linked hand-drawn sketches; a high-fidelity prototype will be fully designed, with all the bells and whistles. Don't move to high-fidelity prototypes until you have completed several rounds of user testing and have locked down the overall design of the major elements of the product. Otherwise you will be throwing away dollars unnecessarily on your designer.

TEST YOUR PROTOTYPE

Think of testing your prototype as like test screening a movie. This prototype can look and feel like the real thing, but you will have built it at a fraction of the cost of a full-blown app. The magic of a prototype is that it allows you and your potential customer to feel and touch the product before you build it, which means you can test different ideas, refining different designs and user interface methods. And you can test whether the product is easy to use and understand. All of this will allow you to collect a wealth of knowledge and ideas to feed back into the product.

If you take away one thing from the Hollywood Method, it is this. Test, test and retest your prototype. Sleep on it. Literally holding the prototype in your hands will give you a completely different perspective on your design choices. Being able to put your prototype in the hands of your customers is a mind-blowing experience. When they can see and touch your solution, they are able to provide you with invaluable insights.

I recommend strongly that you prepare for and record these customer–prototype interactions. Have a script ready. Ask them to perform certain activities and talk to you while they are doing them. Initially, do not guide them through the prototype, but allow them to discover it and interact with it for themselves. This will provide you with invaluable initial feedback, and the user experience will demonstrate how easily understood and discoverable your product is. You can then question them and ask for suggestions and feedback.

Testing, adjusting and retesting each prototype — this should be an iterative process. Because producing a prototype is so cheap and fast, you can refine it thoroughly before you move on to the expensive step of building your real product. This is the most important iteration loop of your startup. Spending time developing and refining your prototype and testing it with customers is the essence of a successful startup.

The beauty of using simple prototypes is that they are incredibly cheap to change. You don't have to go back to a software developer. Your customers play with the prototype and say, 'I don't like that button there' or, 'That doesn't make sense to me — I want to do it this way'. You can go back to the drawing board again and again until your prospective customers are delighted with it and tell you they would buy it on the spot if they could.

Don't forget, the purpose of the pre-production phase is to test product/solution fit. Don't get carried away with how sexy your user interface is or how cool your app looks. This is about filling a need that allows customers to get a job done. Your questions during customer testing should be directed at that. Does your solution solve the problem? Does it solve it for them in a unique and valuable way? How could you improve your solution to better solve the problem?

Do not leave this phase until 10 to 20 target customers have tested your prototype, confirmed that the problem you are solving is critical to them and validated that your solution solves that problem for them so well that they would be willing to pay for it. This is not the time to kid yourself. It's much better to stay in this phase until you get verification that you have achieved product/solution fit, because rework now is inexpensive, whereas in the production phase mistakes and rework become increasingly expensive.

Now you are ready for the production phase. At last you can pass the prototype to a developer and say, 'Build that, and only that.'

3. PRODUCTION

If you feel like you have been working on your startup for an eternity without actually building any technology, good! You have been doing something right. Now we have finally come to the phase where you build your product or application.

So let's talk lights, camera, action! Building your app or platform is probably the part of the process you have most looked forward to. While it's the most visible phase, potentially it's also fraught with the most risk. If you've completed a solid pre-production cycle, however, it can be the easiest part of the process. Unlike most first-timers you will be going into the production phase well prepared. You have a desirable value proposition that you have developed in conjunction with your customers. You have embedded that value proposition in a viable business model so you know how you are going to make money. Most importantly, you have built a working prototype that you have refined and developed in collaboration with your customers.

Many founders dread developing technology, mainly because they've never built an app before. It's a black box to them. Developers speak in acronyms, and they aren't necessarily great at communicating with clients, which adds to the mystery and confirms development as a black art. With a great prototype, though, you can navigate through this process a lot more easily.

Your prototype will continue to pay dividends. It helped you work with your customers to create the solution. Now it will become invaluable in communicating what you actually want built by your developers. If you are a non-technical founder, getting a product built can be a minefield — and a time when you can blow a lot of money fast. If you have done your work in pre-production, however, this phase will be fun rather than a nightmare. But before you begin development you have some choices to make. First, who is going to develop your product?

CHOOSING A DEVELOPMENT PATH

The big decision you need to make now is over who is going to build the product. Simply put, you have three choices:

- a technical co-founder
- an in-house development team
- an outsourced development team.

TECHNICAL CO-FOUNDERS

Having a technical co-founder can often be the easy way out. Remember the hacker, hipster and hustler philosophy of co-founders? 'Commercial' co-founders sometimes team up with a 'technical' co-founder, having concluded that this would offer a cheap and easy way of getting the product built. In my experience, this route can be dangerous. While it might seem convenient, your startup will rapidly outgrow a single developer, and most products require a variety of development skills.

This may be controversial, but if you've got the funding, don't give away big slabs of equity to a technical co-founder who can provide you with a short-term solution. I often see this traditional model play out. The startup founders feel they need a technical co-founder, because they need someone to build the app for them cheaply at the beginning. They give away equity for this service. Think about it. You have given away half your company to a technical co-founder, who does development work worth $100 000. You could have paid the same amount to an outside developer. If in the future your company is ultimately worth $4 million, you have essentially paid $2 million of equity for $100 000 worth of work. So unless that technical founder is a technical visionary able to predict with astounding accuracy where a particular market's going, don't give them your equity. If you're using a technical founder only to get around the cost of building your app, that's a bad decision.

IN-HOUSE DEVELOPMENT

In my experience, hiring your own in-house developers is advantageous because you maintain full control over those resources. You could align them to the company's mission by giving them stock options, for example. If they're good, they're going to do a lot of work outside of hours. They may be highly passionate about the project.

The disadvantage of in-house development is that it's very costly to employ developers, and you don't need them all the time. Sure, when your product is launched you are going to need to maintain it. In the early stages, however, I question the value of companies' hiring dozens and dozens of software developers. They really aren't needed. Having developers in-house can also make you lazy because there's a sunk cost. You undermine your discipline because it means you can say, 'Oh look, can you just make this change for me?', rather than having to specify that change in a structured way, and you know it's going to cost an hourly rate. Longer term, there's a benefit to having in-house developers, but in the short term — and certainly in the early stages of a startup — there's little advantage.

OUTSOURCED DEVELOPMENT

It may be heresy in the startup community, but I am a huge believer in outsourced development in the very early stage of product development during the creation of the minimum viable product, which I will explain in a moment.

By outsourced I don't necessarily mean offshore; you can outsource development onshore as well. There's a big advantage in having your development outsourced in the early phase, especially if you've gone through the first two parts of the process thoroughly and you have a fully functional prototype. The typical danger in outsourcing is that you rack up a lot of time and money communicating and specifying your ideas, and developers can still misunderstand what you want. You may have to say, 'No, I didn't want that. I need you to move the button two inches to the left. I need that button to be purple. When I click on this I need it to do that.' I've seen countless hours and dollars spent by founders trying to communicate their needs to outsourced development providers. However, if you've got a fully functional, clickable prototype, you can give it to them and say simply, 'Build this, and exactly this.' You can hand your prototype to three outsource agencies and say, 'Give me a price to build exactly this.' Getting a quote is faster and the risk of deviation is lower.

In the long run, it is better to obtain funding — from bootstrapping perhaps, or from friends, family and fans — to outsource development of your minimal viable product. That's not to say you shouldn't proceed with caution.

Not all outsource developers are created equal. I'm a believer in onshore outsourced development. This means using someone local to you who builds apps day in and day out, so you can check out what they've done. You can probably get the work done cheaper offshore — in the Philippines, Vietnam, India or China, for example — but communication challenges and time zone differences can cause exasperating problems.

Outsource development centres in offshore locations work better for big companies trying to maintain a code base for a corporate app or when you've got an app that's already built and developed. In the early phases of creating your app, you want someone who is close by, someone you can look in the eye and show the prototype to, whose questions you can answer directly. For early-stage startups, onshore outsource development agencies are the very best solution for building their apps.

You need to consider copyright risk too. Of course, this is not just an issue with offshore development. Whenever you use somebody else to develop your app you have to make sure to tie up IP licensing. Pay attention to the contract you use to engage your outsource developer. It's not an area you want to skimp on. These contracts should include what's called an intellectual property (IP) assignment clause, which means that any development that company does for you is entirely yours. If anyone suggests otherwise, that's someone you don't want to be using. Ensure you own the IP. Have a good lawyer review the contract. The last thing you need is to discover that someone else owns the IP for your product!

THE POWER OF THE PROTOTYPE

The old-school way of specifying a piece of software development such as an app is through what's called a functional specification, which is a comprehensive, hundred-page document itemising what certain fields in a database will look like and so on. Wireframes and prototypes are a much better way of communicating information. Whether your developer is in-house or outsourced, they will be very happy if you can hand them your user journeys, wireframes and clickable prototype. Developers love this new type of briefing. It is a breath of fresh air for them. They don't have to guess what you're thinking and they don't have to interpret endless written specifications. They can see it, touch it, feel it. If there's any doubt, they can simply check the prototype to see what screen a button takes them to, which shows them precisely what you want.

DEVELOPING A MINIMUM VIABLE PRODUCT (MVP)

Once you have decided *who* to build with and how you're going to build your app, you can move on to the second aspect of production, which is about *what* to build. For me, this is essentially the product with the minimum number of features that a customer will pay for, also known as the MVP.

The best way to create an MVP is to determine and start with the single most important feature. You will have identified that feature through your testing and interviews with prospective customers. The purpose of the MVP is to deliver enough features to satisfy the early adopters and then to create a feedback and iteration loop that allows you to add further features based on this feedback.

This is where we can take another tip from Hollywood: stick to the script. Consider your prototype as the script for your product. This is why I recommend you spend an inordinate amount of time in the first two phases. Do not deviate from the script. Once you're in production, it's tempting to say, 'Oh, let's just tweak this. Let's just make those changes.' Those changes can be the death of a product.

Be disciplined. 'We're shooting this script. We're building the app as per the prototype.' You have spent all the time you needed to on the prototype, validating it with customers, adjusting it as necessary. Even when you thought it was just as you wanted it, you paused, slept on it. Perhaps then you spent some extra time on it, knowing that once you moved to production, all you'd want was an exact copy of the prototype. Now here you are. You know that making functionality changes at this point is a recipe for disaster. And it's not only founders who give way to this temptation. Developers too will say, 'Look, we could just slip in this extra functionality here.' If they try this, you have to say, 'No, don't do it.'

This kind of discipline is hard. I recommend three ways to maintain self-control. The first is to have investors tie their finance to the production needs of that particular prototype (we spoke in chapter 5 of the risks to startups of overfunding). The second means of self-control is to set yourself a budget for development and be accountable to it. Outsourcing development can help here, especially if it's a fixed-price quote, which means they'll be disciplined and are unlikely to do anything you haven't specified.

The third mechanism is to park any good ideas or tweaks for the sequel. Don't make the changes to the current product, but don't lose them either. Store them somewhere where you can start to form ideas for the next version of the product. You'll want to test those ideas with customers and prioritise them. This is something you'll come back to and consider for a future version, and a future prototype, when you start the cycle again.

DEPLOY YOUR MVP

It is often said that perfection is the enemy of success. The key here is to get your MVP into the hands of your early adopters and start the feedback cycle. This is how you create product/market fit. If you have followed the process you will now have a real working minimum viable product. It is the most powerful tool you can have as a founder, but this is where the real work begins. Up until this point your market has been theoretical. While you have tested your guesses with customers and tried to prove out your assumptions, there is nothing like having a real product to deploy to early adopters.

This is the acid test, where all your planning and preparation will come to fruition (or not). How do customers feel about your product? Did you hit the mark? Are early adopters coming on board quickly? Are you finding it easy to get customers to pay? If the answer to these questions is no, then you have not yet achieved product/market fit.

You need to continue to iterate, testing and learning from customer feedback, until you achieve product/market fit. This must happen before you run out of money. The beauty behind this method is that you get 'more shots on goal'. The process you have followed up to this point should have got you maximum 'bang for buck', meaning you spent the minimum amount of money to prove out your assumptions.

DO NOT PASS GO!

Regardless of how much funding you have, or how enthusiastic your early customers are, do not move on until you are certain of product/market fit. It's tempting to start hiring salespeople and scaling your organisation. Don't do it! Marc Andreessen sees startups as essentially having two lives: before achieving product/market fit and after achieving product/market fit. He goes further to argue that product/market fit is all that matters. You can screw up a lot of things if customers are beating a path to your door because you are meeting a burning need.

It doesn't really matter what you think — the market is the ultimate test of product/market fit. You just can't hide from it, much as you might like to sometimes. For Andreessen, 'The market needs to be fulfilled and the market will be fulfilled, by the first viable product that comes along.'

The market is always right.

If you haven't achieved product/market fit, go back to the previous phase until you do. Scaling before achieving fit equals death for a startup. You will just throw good money after bad, and you will be distracted by building and operating a company, rather than focusing on achieving fit.

PIVOTING

So what happens if your initial hypothesis (guess) is proven wrong? Well, if you have come to this point quickly and cost-effectively, you may have enough capital to pivot — but only if you have a reasonable alternative to pivot to.

Think of a pivot as plan B. During the course of your experiments with customers it may be that you realise the problem you are solving is not important enough, but that you have discovered a better, bigger problem to solve. Or alternatively, your initial solution to a problem just didn't cut it, but by involving customers in the process you have thought of a better way to solve it. A pivot is just that — redefining the problem or addressing it with a different solution or technology. Your ability to pivot will depend on how quickly you come to the realisation that your business model is not working and that you don't have product/market fit. If you recognise it (and can prove it) early enough, you can adjust course and move to plan B. It all comes down to how much runway you have. Some of the best startups in the world are the result of a pivot, but it takes a founder and team who aren't deluding themselves to execute it successfully.

4. POST-PRODUCTION

Congratulations! You have achieved product/market fit. That's something a lot of startups never achieve, which isn't necessarily a bad thing. Not every idea is a great one. Hopefully those founders used a phased approach to risk too.

Startups need a value hypothesis and a growth hypothesis. The first three phases, and product/market fit in particular, are about proving your value hypothesis, or how you create value for your customers.

Once this is done, you can start thinking about your growth hypothesis. In the Hollywood Method, the post-production phase is focused on your growth hypothesis. How do you get your product to customers in the most cost-effective and scalable way? Here again, you may need to test and iterate.

While post-production takes its place at the end of the Hollywood Method, it is the beginning of business for your startup. The primary consideration now is your business model. You will have already considered numerous questions around how to push you and your product forward: How are you going to market? Are you going to sell your product online or sell it directly using a sales team? Are you going to use channels and partners to do that? How will you sell it? Will it be by subscription or is it going to be free, using a freemium model? All of these questions should have been answered already in your business model using the techniques we have covered.

GET, KEEP AND GROW CUSTOMERS

Being scalable is easier than ever, thanks to the internet. Think how app stores have made products available to millions, thanks to Apple. That infrastructure means startups can now promote, bill and distribute their apps really easily to customers globally. And they can do so without the cost of employing hundreds of salespeople in every corner of the globe.

I have emphasised that you must have product/market fit before scaling, but this doesn't mean you can't start experimenting with customer acquisition strategies, as long as you don't scale them initially. So while your outsourced developer is cutting code, you can start testing go-to-market strategies. You can put up a webpage. You can even pre-sell your product and gauge your audience's interest in it. This is where understanding basic sales and marketing techniques is valuable. Is it a business-to-business or a business-to-consumer product? Each requires a different marketing strategy.

Pricing your product and determining the most effective sales channels are critical for a startup; in fact they can determine if a startup lives or dies.

In his seminal work *Zero to One*, Peter Thiel (co-founder of PayPal and legendary VC) discusses the importance of getting your sales model right. In essence, he suggests the sales strategy you use should be driven heavily by your Customer Acquisition Cost (CAC), a concept discussed in chapter 4. Matching your go-to-market (GTM) strategy with your CAC is crucial. In short, the higher your product is priced, the more you can spend on acquiring the sale. Having these two elements in proportion is important. Are you attacking the large corporate market, with an appropriately high price? Then you can afford to take on a costly direct sales team. Are you attacking the consumer market with a freemium or low monthly subscription cost? Then you need to be acquiring these customers relatively cheaply, and your CAC should reflect this. The danger is when they are mismatched — for example, selling a low-priced product requiring high touch into the corporate market.

Thiel also believes there is a dead zone for pricing — between $100 and $1000 — where it's hard to create either a low cost/volume strategy or a high cost/complex strategy. Sitting in the middle can mean that you cannot find a cost-effective distribution mechanism for your product.

SCALING

Another concept startups need to understand is scaling. I see too many startups fail because they scale too early. One consideration is cost scaling. Most people think of scaling as just going out and hiring 30 people. Money starts coming in and they rush to scale by moving into bigger offices. They think scale is about the size of the cost base. This is a huge misunderstanding. There's no point in hiring 20 salespeople if the customer delivery won't scale.

The most attractive businesses are the ones that scale asymmetrically so the revenue or the customer delivery side scales disproportionally to the cost base. You don't want to grow your startup symmetrically so every time you add a dollar of revenue, you add a dollar of cost. You actually want to be able to add $100 or $1000 of revenue for every dollar of cost. That's why when you think of businesses that are immensely scalable, such as Uber, you ask, 'Okay, can Uber add a new country to its infrastructure, or 200 000 more riders?' And you can answer yes, because Uber doesn't have to hire another 200 sales-people in order to deliver that additional capacity. They can simply use the technology to scale.

Cloud-based services, CRM and software delivered as a service over the internet are all highly scalable businesses because they can deliver increased value and capacity to clients without necessarily having to grow their cost base. Timing is also incredibly important to scaling. This is because if you scale up the cost base too early without having understood what that magic connection is to the customer scale, you're going to go out of business. If you scale your costs and your client-side acquisition or the customer revenue strategy isn't scaling accordingly, then you're never going to make a profit.

Services businesses are an example of a business model that doesn't typically scale. Businesses like accounting firms, law firms and professional service consultants don't scale because they need people to deliver the service. So the parts of your business that will scale the least are the parts that require the most human interaction, while the parts that are going to scale the most are the ones that are predominantly technology driven.

RECAP

Among the 92 per cent of startup failures, 'no market need' is the predominant cause in 32 per cent of cases. How do you ensure there's a market need? You go out and ask the market. You seek to understand your customer — who they are and what they are trying to achieve — and you build a value proposition that responds to that information, ensuring that you make a product customers want and need.

The four steps of the Hollywood Method are designed to ensure that you have a structured roadmap to follow, and that roadmap gives the most possible chances of success at achieving product/market fit. Remember, your startup basically has two phases — before and after product/market fit — and the method outlined in this chapter gives you a greater number of chances of achieving fit before your startup capital runs out.

WHAT'S NEXT

Capital raising is the bane of most startup founders. They often feel they are locked into a never-ending cycle of capital raising and are frustrated by investors who are reluctant to commit. Capital is the oxygen of a startup. In the final chapter I will discuss the 5 Ps of funding fitness — investor personas, proof points, preparation, the pitch and the process.

CHAPTER 9
FUNDING FITNESS

I have spoken a lot in this book about how capital (cash) is the oxygen of your startup. Without it you won't survive. Raising capital — ensuring you secure the right amount from the right people at the right time — is one of the founder's most important roles. If you do it right, it will provide the platform for your startup to flourish.

As a founder and VC, I am often asked my views on the best way to raise capital. This chapter outlines my thoughts on fundraising for startups (what I call funding fitness), and in particular taking an investor-centred design approach to your raise. It is not intended to be a comprehensive authority on capital raising. Rather, I will share some of the valuable lessons I have learned from many years of raising millions of dollars from both private and public investors. I will focus on private capital raising. While there are commonalities between the private and public approaches, the complexities of public capital raising are beyond the scope of this book.

WHAT IS INVESTOR-CENTRED DESIGN?

One of the core principles of the Hollywood Method is to take a human-centred design approach to understanding your customer. As discussed in the previous chapter, by putting your customer at the centre of your product design process and by developing great empathy for them, you create a product and value proposition that is desirable, relevant and feasible. This is the basis of design thinking.

Investor-centred design means applying this same approach to your potential investors. Many founders take a 'shotgun approach' to fundraising — treating all investors much the same and not giving too much thought to what outcome the investor is trying to achieve. As a result, their success is hit and miss. By empathising with your investor you are far more likely to build an investment value proposition that resonates with them, and you far more likely to persuade them to invest in you now and in the future.

The benefits are clear. Firstly, raising capital is time consuming and distracting. The less time you must spend raising capital, the more you can spend on the main event, which is leading and running your startup. I have seen startups caught in 'capital-raising hell', their cap raise dragging on for months and months — heavily affecting their business — until ultimately it goes 'cold', as investors start to think something is wrong with the business or the founder.

Secondly, by applying this process you will attract a better quality of investor, and the right investor for you and your startup. Not all investors are created equal, and while some founders believe that money is money, getting the right investors can provide you with more than just the cash: they can bring useful networks that can make your life so much easier. Choosing the right investor also decreases the risk of investor disharmony, one of the 10 main reasons why startups fail.

There are five key elements of the Funding Fitness model (figure 9.1):

1. persona — choosing the right investor
2. proof — what investors look for

3. prep — preparing for the raise

4. pitch — your investment value proposition

5. process — driving a successful outcome.

When each of these elements is considered and executed on, a startup has significantly more chance of raising capital at the best possible valuation from the best possible investors in the shortest possible time.

FIGURE 9.1: FUNDING FITNESS

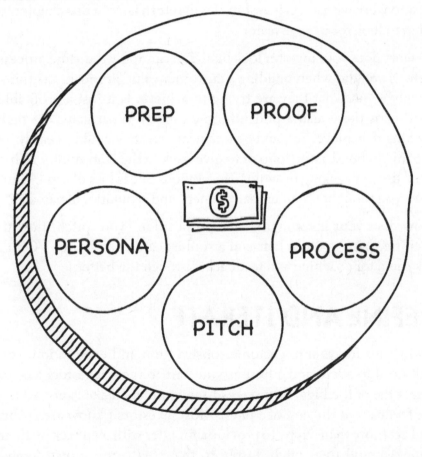

BUILDING INVESTOR EMPATHY

So how do you develop investor empathy? The same way you build customer empathy — by getting out of the building and doing your research. Start by building a profile or persona of your ideal investor. What do they look like? Apart from money, what else do you need to support and grow your business? And before you say Marc Andreessen, think carefully. Different kinds of investors will be a better fit at different stages of your startup. It's not always great to have a huge VC invest in you early. In the early stages, it is sometimes best to work with angel investors. I will return later in this chapter to what to look for in an investor.

So what does your investor look like? You can apply the same process here as you did when building a customer value proposition. Think deeply about what they are trying to achieve. Is it just a profitable 'exit' or is there also a philanthropic aspect? What gains are they looking to achieve? It could be financial, but they could as easily be looking to build a portfolio or to give back to the community. What pain are they seeking to avoid? The obvious one is loss of capital, but have you thought about embarrassment and reputational damage?

How does your investment value proposition (your pitch) fit with their needs? If you can befriend a sophisticated investor or VC and ask them for coaching and feedback, so much the better.

REFINE AND ITERATE

As in your forays into customer observation and exploration, you will need to adapt and adjust as you start to meet investors face to face. One of the biggest mistakes I see founders make is not asking for feedback at the end of a pitch. Most investors I know aren't shy, and are more than happy to provide a founder with feedback on their approach and their pitch. Listen to that feedback — don't defend yourself — then it's back to the lab so you can iterate and refine your value proposition.

PERSONA: WHAT TO LOOK FOR IN AN INVESTOR

You will quickly realise that investors are as diverse as startup founders. Some of them shouldn't be investing in startups at all, and some are veterans with extensive investment success behind them. They fall into four basic categories:

- friends, family and fans (F3)
- angels and super angels
- venture capital funds (VCs)
- institutional investors.

The investors you should focus most of your efforts on are the angels and the VCs. Some VCs are happy to invest early, before your revenue stream has begun, while others will require a particular revenue threshold to be crossed.

Whether you are dealing with an angel or a VC firm, you will ultimately be interacting with an individual. Capital raising is a two-way street. You do your due diligence on them, just as they do their due diligence on you. If they invest in your company you will be interacting with them for a very long time, which makes finding the right investor for you extremely important. So what questions should you ask your potential investor? What are you looking for?

STYLE AND EXPECTATIONS

Investors have different styles and expectations. Find out if they favour a hands-on or hands-off approach. Do they invest in a particular industry sector (such as financial technology, or fintech) or do they prefer a particular type of startup (such as SaaS, or software as a service)? What are their expectations of founders' level of commitment and involvement? Founder salaries? When do they approve of founders taking cash off the table? How patient are they?

What are their views on exit time frames? Do they have a preference for how they exit? Where does their money come from? Is it their own or are they investing someone else's money? There is no right or wrong answer to any of these questions, but by asking them you will start to form a view of how well suited this kind of investor is to you and your company.

EXPERIENCE

I hate to say it, but you will come across a lot of wannabe investors. Just as the startup community attracts founders who like the idea of running a startup but aren't serious, you will meet people who claim to be investors but have never written a cheque. Questions to ask include:

- ► How many deals have they done? Over what time frame?
- ► When did they make their last deal?
- ► Do they lead or co-invest alongside someone else?
- ► Do they follow on or only make single investments?
- ► What is the size of their average cheque?

NETWORK

A great investor will bring more than just money. Ask them:

- ► Do they have experience in your domain?
- ► Can they help with customer referrals?
- ► Are they a former founder? Can they help coach you?
- ► Are they prepared to sit on the advisory or actual board?
- ► Are they connected to other investors?
- ► Can they help close out the round?

Smart founders leverage their investor networks to create an advantage for them. Don't just view your investors as dollar machines.

REFERENCES

When determining whether an investor is right for you, ask around. The startup community is relatively small. Ask a potential investor what other startups they have partnered with and how those investments have gone. Speak to founders who have worked with them. If you respect their anonymity, other founders will tell you the reality of working with a particular investor. Some have better reputations than others. It's important you get third-party validation before you take the money.

PROOF: WHAT INVESTORS LOOK FOR

Just as you are doing your research on your potential investor, they are doing theirs on you. After all, it is their money (or their fund's), and they won't be writing you a cheque without going through their own process.

Founders often ask me what investors look for. Their investment processes — from the heuristic to more analytical approaches — will be as diverse as the investors themselves. Whatever their general approach, most investors look at six key areas when assessing whether a startup is investible:

- ▶ team/founders
- ▶ market
- ▶ plans
- ▶ tech
- ▶ proof
- ▶ terms.

Don't let this overwhelm you. If you have followed the advice in this book, you will already be investor ready and will be well prepared for your investment pitch.

TEAM/FOUNDERS

The importance of the team and the founders cannot be overstated. Previous chapters have prepared you to be a fit founder — one with great levels of self-awareness and maturity. Investors will be sizing you and your team up. Experienced investors know how hard the startup journey can be, so they need to be convinced that the team can go the distance. Are you a leader, and do you have a co-founder team that complements your strengths and weaknesses? They will test your self-awareness to assess whether you are coachable. This is the first thing I look for when I meet a founder I am considering investing in. Uncoachable founders are a nightmare.

Your passion is also important. Are you authentically connected to the problem you are solving? Do you care? Can you demonstrate empathy for the customer? What experience do you have in this field? Why you? They will also look favourably on prior startup experience, whether or not it was successful.

Lastly, and most importantly, do you convey a sense of integrity? Don't bullshit investors. They are thinking about giving you a lot of money. They need to build rapport with you and they need to trust you. You need to demonstrate that you are trustworthy.

MARKET

Know your market. That doesn't mean putting 57 slides in your pitch deck on market size, but it does mean knowing the key sizing statistics in your chosen market. Some investors are detail oriented, others just want a high-level feel. Have the detail available as an appendix if called for. You are looking to communicate the attractiveness of the market and how you intend to take advantage of the market opportunity.

PLANS

If you have done it right, you will have completed a Business Model Canvas and a documented value proposition. You may or may not need to produce these, but again they are useful as an appendix. You will need to understand in detail and speak to your business model — your value proposition and how you will make money.

TECH

Tech is cool. It's shiny. What gets investors excited is unique/ defendable tech or, even better, real technology that has been developed. Nothing is more powerful than a product demonstration. If you have an MVP or a product, demonstrate it early! Don't wait until the end of the pitch. A good product demo tells your story better than you can. If you don't have a working product or MVP, then show your wireframes. Do not pass your wireframes off as a working product. If you don't have wireframes, what are you doing raising money?

PROOF

Proof is the ultimate slam dunk when raising capital. Nothing shuts up a sceptical investor faster than real, cold, hard customer cash! Revenue is the ultimate proof point. Predictable, growing revenue is even better. If you have this, investors will usually beat a path to your door.

If you are at a pre- or early-revenue stage, then early adopters and trial customers are useful. If there is a customer (who is not your brother-in-law) who can speak to an investor and tell them about how your product solves their problem, that is awesome.

There are a multitude of other potential proof points. What investors are trying to determine here is, 'Has the market spoken?' Startups are built on a lot of assumptions. Which of those assumptions has the market proven true for you?

TERMS

There are heaps of great resources and books you can consult to help you understand the best deal terms. A quick acid test for a lot of investors is to ask you how much money you are raising and on what valuation.

Nothing signals an amateur founder and kills an investor's interest faster than an unrealistic valuation. If you don't know how to value your company, do your research on current market valuations before starting the capital-raising process. There is certainly plenty of room for negotiation, and many strategies for maximising your valuation, but if you serve up an insane, unsupported valuation in your first meeting with an investor, they will usually put you in the 'thanks but no thanks' category.

The same is true of claiming your capital raise is 'oversubscribed', meaning more people want to fund you than you need. 'Hooray! You have reached startup nirvana. Then why are you talking to me?' Shortly I will discuss the importance of keeping momentum in your capital raise, but what I don't mean is trying to create a false sense of urgency. Treat your investors with respect and they will do the same for you.

Myth: I'm the boss!

Control. It's something founders obsess about. There is a myth that by starting your own company you will have complete control. It's true there is a lot of flexibility in running a startup, which makes it far more exciting for some than the corporate world. The minute you take on outside capital, however, you become answerable to investors, and in most instances to a board. If you expect to be able to make every decision independently, you will be disappointed!

Some founders want to take an investor's money but don't want the investor involved in the business in any capacity. You may be able to negotiate this with your early angel investors. As individuals, they can make their own decisions about the risk of taking a hands-off approach to their investment in your company. But this will not happen with any serious VC. They cannot write you a blank cheque with other people's money, then allow you to proceed without any oversight or control measures. That's why it's crucial to choose your investors wisely and to be respectful of their hard-earned capital.

The only way to remain completely in control of your destiny is not to take any outside money at all. Frankly, that is going to limit your options for growth. Much better is to establish a collaborative approach with your investors and set up a framework for reporting and governance that will provide them with confidence and insight into the business. They have experience and networks to help your business succeed. Make your investors part of the team and bring them along for the journey.

PREPARATION: START BEFORE YOU START

Remember your ABC — always be closing. One thing you can do to dramatically improve the odds of a successful capital raise is to create awareness of your startup within the investment community *before* you actually need to raise capital. This usually means some level of PR. I also recommend holding awareness meetings: meet with your target investors before your capital raise solely for the purpose of getting your company on their radar. This way, they can get familiar with your startup without the pressure of a raise. Don't ask for money. In fact, specifically say you are not raising capital at the moment although you will be in the future. The purpose of this meeting is simply to make them familiar with your business. They can get to know you and your team, and you will look so much more professional and in control. It's refreshing to meet a startup founder who is not raising capital.

CREATE A DATA ROOM

Just before starting the process create a data room. A data room should be a secure online location (such as Dropbox) that contains all the important documents an investor will need. These should include, at a minimum:

- your pitch deck
- an information memorandum (your formal offer document)
- company legal documents (constitution, shareholder's agreement etc.)
- key financial reports (P&L, balance sheets etc.)
- your 12-month financial forecast
- your Business Model Canvas
- any material customer contracts
- anything else that would be relevant to an investor.

Compile and update this information early, before commencing the capital raise. You do not want to be scrambling for this information mid raise. Be prepared.

PITCH: YOUR INVESTOR VALUE PROPOSITION

An investor's decision to write you a cheque will depend on many factors. A critical element will be the quality of your pitch. This doesn't just mean the slide deck; it also means how good you are at thinking on your feet and communicating the key aspects of your startup. Remember where we started — investor-centred design. This is the time to reconnect with your investor value proposition and ensure you are communicating investible points during your pitch.

THE PITCH DECK

I have seen hundreds of pitch decks, and most of them were terrible. There is a magic formula for the perfect pitch deck: it should be short (no more than 10 to 12 slides) and it should cover the key aspects investors want to see. What problem are you solving, for whom, and what makes you different? There are endless resources on this. Google some great pitch decks. Remember, this isn't about having flash slides. It's about content — ensuring the investor understands what you are trying to achieve.

This isn't your sales pitch deck; it needs to be investor focused. If you have empathy for your investor, you will be able to tailor your message to address their gains, pains and needs. Be clear about your use of funds and how long those funds will buy you in terms of runway. There is a standard pitch format that most investors expect. Do your research and conform to it.

MOVE OVER, DON DRAPER

The way you pitch will depend largely on your personal style. If you aren't comfortable presenting, then it's time to learn. Practise, practise, practise. Understand that you don't have to do this alone. Use your team to assist you in the pitching process. That doesn't mean having them sit there and look pretty; it means having them actively involved in the pitch. Your CTO might demonstrate the product, for example, or you could share the pitch between co-founders. If you get this right it will show investors that your team has depth and breadth, and that they aren't investing in just a single talented founder.

This is also an opportunity for an investor to get to know you as a person. Pitching provides an opportunity for you to show a clear, authentic connection to the problem. Your passion should shine through. Why should they invest in you and in this startup? Why should they invest now? Be yourself, be authentic and above all be honest. Nothing sinks a pitch faster than a founder who tries to bullshit. It's important to be realistic. There is no need to exaggerate the opportunity, your performance or your product. A well-researched investor will be realistic and will get to the truth pretty quickly. It's vital that they can trust you and that you show maturity.

Lastly, the best thing you can do in a pitch is listen. Ask questions and listen to the responses. Listen to what the investor has to say. Don't feel the need to immediately respond to or defend against criticism. Ask them why they have formed a particular view. I have seen countless founders screw up a pitch by just jumping head first into their formal pitch — and immediately losing the investor.

At the completion of the pitch be sure to answer any open questions or commit to following up on anything you need to research. Always ask for feedback on your pitch. I don't mean try to hard close the investor; I mean genuinely ask for suggestions on how it could be improved. The feedback could be valuable and it shows you are coachable. Also, it is totally acceptable to ask for introductions or referrals to other investors. Your startup might not fit their investment profile but they will doubtless know someone who could be a better fit for you. Ask for the referral, and follow up when you say you will.

PROCESS: OWN IT!

The best advice I can give you when it comes to raising capital is to *own the process*. What I mean by that is to proactively get out in front of it. Anticipate when you will need to raise capital, plan for it and manage the process.

TIMING

There is a right and a wrong time to raise capital. You want to be raising capital from a position of strength, not of weakness, so timing is important. The best time to raise capital is when you don't need it. This may sound obvious, but I see a lot of startups begin the process too late and end up in a position of desperation. Others delay capital raising in the hope that their business metrics will improve and they will get a better valuation. When you are desperate you will take poor deal terms, or poor investors. The ideal time for a raise is when you have more than six months of capital runway and your business has hit one or more key proof points.

It's also very important to allow enough time for your capital raise. The reason for that is that it takes a long time to identify, meet and close all the potential investors. They'll be busy, hard to reach. People will jerk your chain and say they'll invest but back down when you ask them to write a cheque, so you're going to have investors fall through. It's a long process, even just getting to the point where you have built a book that identifies who is willing to invest and at what rates. Even when you have an agreement in principle, the process itself — executing the documents, drawing up the subscription agreements, getting people to sign shareholder agreements — takes time. Getting people from the start of the process to depositing money in your account takes between three and six months.

BUILD A BOOK

This may be controversial, but I firmly believe you should have a formal timetable for your capital raise. This will allow for:

- an investor roadshow
- an offer period
- opening of the book (opening of bids for stock)
- closing of the book (closing of bids for stock)
- final stock allocations.

While this approach is typically used by public companies, I think it is of huge value in private company capital raising too. Setting specific start and finish dates for your raise creates a structure and then allows you to move on. It's efficient and well understood in the investment community.

So why isn't it adopted by more startups when they raise? Because it's a risk. You put yourself out there, and if you have not done your preparation, or if your company is not strong, then you will get to the end of the process without having raised the capital. This can be embarrassing. To avoid it, many startups maintain an open-ended cycle for capital raising, which ends only when they find investors. It can be a painfully long march.

My suggestion is this. Spend four weeks preparing your company. Get your pitch done. Get your data room set up. Start building a list of investors. Put those investors into a CRM (customer relationship manager) — my personal preference is Pipedrive. Manage the process like a sales campaign.

Start by building a prospect list. The bigger the list of target investors the better. Over the next four weeks, contact and meet all of them as part of an investor roadshow. By concentrating your investor meetings, you will improve your pitch incrementally and be able to incorporate feedback and gauge interest. At the end of the roadshow you can make a launch decision based on the feedback and reception you received from investors. It's important at this point not to delude yourself. Don't be afraid to qualify your investors hard. It's better to get a fast no and move on. If the reception was positive and you think you have a lead investor, then push the button and open the book.

By this stage your investors should be well prepared. By establishing a formal offer period (with open and close dates between which you will take bids for stock), you will create a sense of urgency. If there really is good demand for your startup, then this will spur your investors into action and they will give your deal priority. You may even end up in the enviable situation of being oversubscribed.

DOING THE DEAL

Once you have completed your roadshow and have your investors primed, it's time to get the deal done. There are plenty of resources out there to help you here, and having a great lawyer is an important first step. Find a lawyer who has done capital raising for startups before. You don't need a big-name firm; you need someone who does this kind of work every day. Ask fellow founders for referrals, and do your homework.

In getting a deal over the line it's important to be realistic. While there is always give and take, there will be generally accepted market norms in your region or sector. There will be valuation ranges based on stage and traction, and control terms and other items that are perfectly reasonable. Again, ask around and find out what the last few cap raises looked liked for businesses like yours. If you are asking for terms outside of the norm (a very high valuation, for example), then you better be prepared to justify it.

Lastly, the importance of a lead or cornerstone investor cannot be overstated. A lead investor is someone with whom you have a strong connection, someone prepared to put up the majority of the capital in a particular round. A lead is important for two reasons: (1) they typically price and validate the round, and (2) they can help drag along the other minor investors to complete the round.

If you can lock in the right lead investor, your life is going to be much easier and your capital raise will proceed a lot more smoothly. Depending on the size of the round, a good lead will be putting in 50 per cent or more of the capital you are raising. A few larger investors are usually easier to manage than many smaller ones. Your lead investor will usually put down a term sheet that prices the round (proposes a valuation) and outlines the other major deal terms. This doesn't mean you shop the term sheet, but it does make it far easier for you to have conversations with other investors, as you now have a benchmark and validation.

Any lead investor will also often have other smaller VCs or angels they co-invest with. Once you get them on board they can usually use their network to close out the balance of the round. It is in the lead's best interests for your round to close fast, so they will help you. Treat all your investors well, but treat your lead investor especially well.

Myth: Valuation is the scoreboard

As a wise man once said to me, 'You can't eat shares!' The value of your startup is interesting, but it isn't the only thing. The value of a startup is often a hot topic of discussion. Startup XYX just raised $10 million. On what valuation, most will ask? High valuations often mean bragging rights for founders and are held out as the scoreboard. Building a sustainable, profitable company is more important than your valuation. There is a natural tension between founders and investors. When it comes to valuation, there is always downward pressure from investors and upward pressure from founders.

Entrepreneurs often have an unrealistic view of how much their startup is worth. That can create a lot of conflict between investors and founders and can become a huge sticking point in capital-raising negotiations. I have seen valuation negotiations sink startups in their early stages. So you need to have a realistic assessment of your company's value. It's not the be-all and end-all, and it's not the scoreboard. The only valuation that matters is the one placed on the company when you exit.

Remember, most startups won't even make it to an exit, so squabbling over valuation at an early stage is mostly academic. Everyone needs to be aligned around a fair valuation. That means founders believe they own enough of the company to feel rewarded for their sweat, and investors own enough of the company for their capital and the risk they are taking. If investors and entrepreneurs don't agree on the value of the company, it is unlikely you will get a capital raise anyway, and if you do, then one party will feel disgruntled and won't be pushing as hard as they can for the success of the business.

RECAP

Raising capital is part of being a founder, although it's usually something founders dread. If you follow an investor-centred design approach, and if you apply the same techniques that you used to develop your customer value proposition to develop your investor value proposition, then the process can actually be enjoyable and rewarding.

Don't approach capital raising with the loose, unstructured approach used by many startups. Prepare yourself and your startup before you begin. Get your pitch down and your data room in order. Then run a time-bound structured process. Create momentum and a sense of urgency by owning the process from start to finish.

Treat your investors with respect. Listen to them and be prepared to adapt in response to their feedback. If they don't invest in this round, it doesn't mean they won't invest in the next.

Prepared, investor-ready startups raise more capital, at better terms, faster and more easily than those that take an unstructured approach.

FINAL THOUGHTS

In 1914 the larger part of a factory owned by iconic inventor Thomas Edison burnt to the ground. Edison's reaction was priceless. As the fire still raged he turned to his son and said, 'Go get your mother and all her friends. They will never see a fire like this!' Instead of viewing the fire as an unmitigated disaster, the end of the line, Edison saw it as a chance to rebuild, to start afresh. In the years that followed, Edison was more focused and successful than ever.

After reading this book you may think that startup is practically synonymous with failure, and there is some truth in this. The numbers don't lie. By applying the strategies I have outlined in this book you will be better placed to succeed, yet as a startup founder you need to brace yourself for dealing with failure. The most successful entrepreneurs know that failure is actually part of the game. My favourite entrepreneur, Gary Vaynerchuk, sees it like this: just as there is no 'undefeated' fighter in UFC, 'there is no undefeated in entrepreneurship'.

So let me leave you with a bonus hack for dealing with environments that are susceptible to a lot of failure and a great deal of stress: *stoicism*. Author and entrepreneur Tim Ferris describes stoicism as the ultimate 'personal operating system' for high-stress environments.

Stoicism is a school of philosophy that was popular in the Greek and Roman worlds for more than 500 years up to the third century AD. With a core principle of personal ethics, it teaches how to turn adversity into opportunity. Recently stoicism has had something of a rebirth, in Silicon Valley — for good reason. It provides a unique lens through which startup founders can reframe their obstacles.

When speaking to founders I simplify stoicism into three major principles:

- **Seek to control only what you *can* control.** A lot of founder stress is generated by their imagination or by things they have no control over. As a founder, you can control only three things: your perceptions (what things mean), your actions (what energy you apply to your daily activities) and your will (your discipline and commitment to thrive under duress).

- **Respond, don't react.** Many founders I know are passionate and emotional. If you only react to a situation, you apply the past to the present. Rather, respond unemotionally to the data you are seeing now without viewing it through a historical lens.

- **The obstacle is the way.** Change your perception of adversity. By testing yourself and facing your fears you can use these challenges to grow and develop.

There is so much more to stoicism than I can share here, but, as many founders to whom I have introduced it have discovered, it is a valuable tool for reframing startup failure and adversity.

Our world needs disruptive technology startups because they are the engine that drives science, art, health, transport and so much else *forward*. I believe that founders who are fostered and developed will go on to achieve great things and make the world a better place. I want to help create an environment in which founders can take risks safely within a clear structure knowing they will find physical, mental and emotional support during their journey.

YOU ARE NOT ALONE

The commonest concern I hear from experienced founders and entrepreneurs is that their world can be a lonely place. I began this book by noting my obsession for helping to guide founders and to build a venture ecosystem that better supports them. I encourage you to get in touch with me. I would love to hear your thoughts on this book and how it has changed the way you approach your startup ventures. If you want to reach me personally, I can be found on Instagram (@jamiepride) or on the web (www.jamiepride.com)

If you think you are funding fit and want to pitch me, get in touch with my venture arm, Phi Digital Ventures, at www.phidv.com, but make sure you have applied the 5 Ps of funding fitness before you do!

If you are inspired to work more on your founder fitness, I encourage you to reach out to The Founder Lab, at www.thefounderlab.com.au. Our goal is to apply the principles outlined in this book to develop and train world-class founders.

And remember, there are no answers in the building — so get out there and take some risks.

ACKNOWLEDGEMENTS

Firstly this book wouldn't have been possible without my family, Sam, Phoebe, Harrison and Imogen, who have been there through all the ups and downs. Words cannot express how much your support has meant to me.

To my mum, Sandra, who sacrificed a lot and pushed me hard so I could do what I am able to do today. I love you.

A big thank you to the team at Wiley: Lucy Raymond, who believed in this book; Chris Shorten, who made it happen; and most importantly, Jem Bates, my editor.

I have had a lot of help along the way from awesome thought leaders: Kath Walters, without whom this book would never have happened; Matt Church, who has been a constant mentor and inspiration; Janine Garner, Dan Gregory, Yamini Naidu, Angela Lockwood and Jack Delosa. Thank you for your sound advice and encouragement.

To the legal eagles, who have saved my arse on many an occasion: Fiona Shand, Tim Flahvin and Peter Hodges, thanks for your patience, support and amazing work, and for giving me the airspace to get this done.

My co-founder at The Founder Lab, Con Georgiou, has been a huge influence on this book. His passion for founders is a constant inspiration. Thanks, bud.

I want to make special mention of the investors who have supported me through the tough times: Josh Best, Adam Powick, James Spenceley and Grant Schaffer.

To the misfits: Dan Adair (for kicking my arse); the Chairman (who taught me you can't eat shares); Jessica Glenn (who gives me my dose of geek); Mia Vassallo (analyst extraordinaire); and Tim Philips (who listens to my constant ramblings).

The entrepreneurial journey is never an easy one. And I have had my share of highs and lows. Over the years a few people apart from my family have been there for me when the chips were down: Nate DeBritt, my best mate and a rock of support; Sean O'Meara, the most driven entrepreneur I know, a good friend and someone who has shared my journey; Tristan Walker, who was there when it mattered; Mike Tzetlin, who listened; and Jeremy Bond, whose unwavering support got me through some tough times. I cannot thank you all enough.

Lastly, to all the amazing founders I have had the privilege of working with. I am constantly amazed and inspired by you.

INDEX

There are moments in life when you step up. Starting you're own business is one of the biggest. It's rare to find the few who will and rarer still to find a mentor who has. Jamie has and in *Unicorn Tears* he shows us how to avoid failure and crush it in business.

— **Matt Church**, founder of ThoughtLeaders, author of
Next: thriving in the decade of disruption

Unicorn Tears has it all; why businesses fail, how to succeed, and how to enjoy the journey. All presented by one of the countries most respected entrepreneurs and investors. This is a must read.

— **Jack Delosa**, CEO and founder of The Entourage

If you are a startup, thinking about becoming one, or simply interested in the idea of entrepreneurialism and how to maximise your chances of success, as opposed to becoming one of the 92 per cent that fails, then Jamie's book, *Unicorn Tears*, is a must-read. Jam-packed with how to's and ideas, and supported with his own stories and those of others, *Unicorn Tears*, is essential reading for anyone serious about startup success.

— **Janine Garner**, speaker, mentor, author of *It's Who You Know*

We live in a world where expertise is all too readily claimed and the academic world has become, well, a little bit 'academic'. This is what makes Jamie Pride's observations so valuable — his knowledge and wisdom has been earned through experience in real world conditions with numerous startups. He makes me want to be a better entrepreneur — and every time we speak, he helps me do just that.

— **Dan Gregory**, CEO, The Impossible Institute